Administrative Law

Round Hall's Nutshell, Nutcase, Exam Focus, and Legal Skills Series

NUTSHELL TITLES

Specially written for students of Irish law, each title in the **Nutshell Series** from Round Hall is an accessible review of key principles, concepts and cases. Nutshells are both the ideal introductory text, and the perfect revision aid.

- **Administrative Law** by Matthew Holmes
- **Company Law** – 3rd edition by Catherine McConville
- **Contract Law** by Fergus Ryan
- **Constitutional Law** – 2nd edition by Fergus Ryan
- **Criminal Law** – 3rd edition by Cecilia Ní Choileáin
- **Equity and Trusts** – 2nd edition by Miriam Dowling
- **Employment Law** by Dorothy Donovan
- **Evidence** by Ross Gorman
- **Family Law** by Louise Crowley
- **The Irish Legal System** by Dorothy Donovan
- **Land Law** – 2nd edition by Ruth Cannon
- **Succession Law** by Karl Dowling and Robert Grimes
- **Tort** – 2nd edition by Ursula Connolly

NUTCASE TITLES

Round Hall Nutcases are written to give you the key facts and principles of **important cases** in core legal subject areas. Straightforward, no-nonsense language makes Nutcases an easy way to understand and learn key cases.

- **Criminal Law** by Majella Walsh
- **Evidence** by Neil Van Dokkum
- **Tort** – 2nd edition by Val Corbett

EXAM FOCUS TITLES

The series is especially designed to support students in the weeks coming up to exams by providing a unique tutorial approach to answering questions.

- **Criminal Law** by Sarah Carew

LEGAL SKILLS TITLES

The Legal Skills Series helps students master the essential legal and research skills needed to succeed in their studies and in their future careers.

- **How to Think, Write and Cite: Key Skills for Irish Law Students** by Jennifer Schweppe, Ronan Kennedy, Larry Donnelly and Dr Elaine Fahey.

NUTSHELLS

Administrative Law

by

MATTHEW HOLMES
BCL, LLM (KCL)
Barrister-at-Law

ROUND HALL  THOMSON REUTERS

Published in 2014 by
Thomson Reuters (Professional) Ireland Limited
(Registered in Ireland, Company No. 80867. Registered Office
and address for service 43 Fitzwilliam Place, Dublin 2)
trading as Round Hall.

Print origination by Carrigboy Typesetting Services

Printed and bound by
CPI Group (UK) Ltd, Croydon, CR0 4YY

ISBN 978–0–41403–480–8

This book is dedicated to my family:

Micheal and Dympna and my sister Bairbre, and in loving memory of mo dhaideo, Uinseann.

Preface

It is my hope that this book will be of use to all who buy it and will provide insight into Irish administrative law. Those who steal it will hopefully be provided with insight into Irish criminal law (and up to 10 years inside the most antiquated prison system in Western Europe).

The number of people who have helped me with this book, my legal studies and my legal career is so large that the list would probably be longer than the book itself. Special thanks must be reserved for Shane Costelloe, Dermot Manning and Edmund Sweetman, my former masters. Anything they couldn't teach probably isn't worth knowing.

I must also thank everyone who helped me by proofreading this book: Alice Harrison, Mary Rogan, Alan D.P. Brady, Aideen Keane, Sophie Honohan, Simon Donagh, Stephen McCrea and Eoin Byrne. Their wonderful assistance is very genuinely appreciated and, without it, I could not have finished this work.

Thanks also to: John Dunne, Dolores Keane, Steven Dixon, Siobhán Ní Chúlacháin, Nicola Munnelly, Eoin Gallagher, Edel Gilligan, James O'Brien, Shaun Smyth, Jennifer Morgan, Séamus Clarke, Tony McGillicuddy, John Noonan, Keith Rooney, Clara Connolly, Bebhin Sparks, Dr Peter Keenan, Michael Reynolds, Adam Brophy and everyone from Round Hall, the staff and faculties of the schools of law in UCD and King's College London, the Irish Medico-Legal Society, the committees of the 97th and 98th sessions of UCD Law Society, and last, but not least, the Zoo Crew.

This book represents the law as I understand it as of September 2013.

Contents

Table of Cases

ADMINISTRATIVE LAW

European Court of Justice

European Court of Human Rights

England

ADMINISTRATIVE LAW

Northern Ireland

Australia

Canada

United States

South Africa

Table of Legislation

PRE-1922 STATUTES

IRISH STATUTORY INSTRUMENTS

EU Treaties

European Directives

European Regulations

European Convention on Human Rights

English Statutes

English Statutory Instruments

Canadian Statutes

United States Statutes

International Treaties

ADMINISTRATIVE LAW

Introduction

This book is for law students and lawyers. It is intended to provide an outline of administrative law to the student who is encountering it for the first time and as a revision aid coming up to the dreaded exams. It is also intended to be of use to practising lawyers as a quick reference guide for court. This book is divided into two sections. The first section deals with the procedures administrators should use and what may be considered unfair procedure. The second section deals with judicial review procedure, including: who and what can be judicially reviewed; the procedure by which a judicial review can be taken; and the remedies which can be awarded if it is successful.

Judicial review is a particularly dynamic area of law which is constantly in flux. There have been significant recent changes to judicial review procedure, particularly relating to time limits, due to the Rules of the Superior Courts (Judicial Review) 2011 (S.I. No. 691 of 2011), which came into effect on January 1, 2012. This book endeavours, wherever possible, to rely primarily on Irish authorities, although authorities from foreign jurisdictions are called upon where appropriate.

What is Administrative Law?

Administrative law is the branch of public law which governs the exercise of public powers and duties by administrative decision-makers and bodies, including state agencies and public authorities. It can be considered to be the neighbour of constitutional law. It ensures that public bodies carry out their functions in accordance with the law, whereas constitutional law is concerned with principles and policy. In particular, administrative law deals with the power of the courts to control the actions of state agencies and public authorities by reviewing their actions or decisions in the process known as judicial review. The principal source of administrative law is common law, which is developed on a case-by-case basis. However, administrative law has been added to by statute. As public law, it deals with the relationship between individuals and the State, as opposed to private law (like contract law) which deals with relationships between private individuals. Three key principles which underlie administrative law are:

INTRODUCTION

1. every executive or administrative act that affects rights or interests must be legal;
2. every entity, including the Government and its servants, is subject to the rule of law; and
3. the legality of executive or administrative acts is determined by an independent judiciary.

What is Judicial Review?

Judicial review is a type of court proceeding where a judge of the High Court reviews the lawfulness of a decision or an action of the inferior courts, tribunals and a wide variety of other administrators. It is a remedy exclusive to the High Court, with appeals being taken to the Supreme Court. Judicial reviews are a challenge to the way in which a decision has been made, rather than to the final decision. Judicial review is concerned with ensuring that the correct procedures have been followed rather than the substance or merits of the conclusion reached. The reviewing court will not substitute what it thinks is the "correct" decision—if the rightness or wrongness of a result is being challenged, then an appeal is a better avenue of relief. The court in a judicial review has the power to:

(a) quash a decision using the relief know as "certiorari";
(b) direct that a certain course of action be taken using the relief known as "mandamus";
(c) inquire into the credentials of a person in authority using the relief known as "*quo warranto*";
(d) prevent an action from being taken with the relief known as "prohibition";
(e) grant certain orders known as injunctions;
(f) state that the parties have certain rights using the relief known as a declaration;
(g) award financial compensation known as "damages";
(h) direct the release of a person held in custody with the remedy known as "habeas corpus".

Clarke J. explained the principles underlying judicial review in the recent decision of *Rawson v Minister for Defence* [2012] IESC 26 as follows:

"It is trite law to say that judicial review is concerned with the lawfulness of decision making in the public field. Where a decision is made by a public person or body which has the force of law and which affects the rights and obligations of an individual then it hardly needs to be said that the courts have jurisdiction to consider whether the decision concerned is lawful. If it were not so then it is hard to see how such a situation would be consistent with the rule of law. For if decisions materially affecting the rights and obligations of individuals could be made in an unlawful fashion the rule of law would not be upheld.

While the circumstances in which a decision made by a public person or body may be found to be unlawful are varied, it is possible to give a non-exhaustive account of the principal bases by reference to which such a finding might be made. First, the decision must be within the power of the person or body concerned. Second, the process leading to the decision must comply both with fair procedures and with whatever procedural rules may be laid down by law for the making of the decision concerned. Third, the decision maker must address the correct question or questions which need to be answered in order to exercise the relevant power and in so doing must have regard to any necessary factors properly taken into account and must also exclude any considerations not permitted. Fourth, in answering the proper questions raised and in assessing all matters properly taken into account the decision maker must come to a rational decision in the sense in which that term is used in the *jurisprudence*. There may, of course, be many variations or additions to that very broad description of the matters that need to be assessed in order to decide whether a decision affecting rights and obligations has been lawfully made."

Fennelly J. had this to say about judicial review in the subsequent Supreme Court decision of *Mallak v Minister for Justice* [2012] IESC 59:

"The phenomenon that is the modern law of judicial review, though rooted in history, has witnessed extraordinary development over the past thirty years. At its heart it insists that ... any administrative decision ... must be bona fide held and factually sustainable and not unreasonable. The underlying principles of judicial review are universal. Courts of the common law have developed and expanded the historic rules of natural justice, in more recent times with inspiration from international human-rights instruments such as the European Convention on Human Rights and, in this jurisdiction, from the Constitution. The Court of Justice of the European Union speaks of a 'complete system of legal remedies' ... The rules are composed of a number of inter-related features, the underlying fundamental presumption being that those to whom discretionary powers are entrusted will exercise them fairly insofar as they may affect individuals. Where fairness can be shown to be lacking, the law provides a remedy. The right of access to the courts is an indispensable cornerstone of a State governed by the rule of law."

JUDICIAL REVIEW, THE SEPARATION OF POWERS AND THE STATE

Ireland, like most other democracies, is governed using the separation of powers model. This means that the State's powers are vested in three different institutions—the legislature (which has the power to create, amend and repeal laws); the executive (which is responsible for the daily administration of the State); and the judiciary (which interprets and applies the laws). The Irish Constitution grants legislative power to the Oireachtas (Art.15), executive power to the Government or its delegates (Art.28), and judicial power to the courts (Art.34). The reason for this separation of powers is to provide a system of checks and balances in the exercise of public power so as to ensure no single branch of the State has too much power.

The reach of the State has grown since the 19th century, particularly during the latter half of the 20th century. Prior to this, the responsibilities of the State were few and classical—the conduct of foreign affairs, upholding the public order and responsibility for the armed forces. The State now impacts on the lives of its citizens in many more ways than it did a century ago. With the invention of the modern welfare State, the citizen now receives services from the State such as education, health care and even accommodation, food and clothing. The State now has responsibility for, inter alia, the regulation of trade and industry, pensions, the planning of how privately-owned land can be used, what substances and objects a person can possess or ingest, and the banking system. In carrying out these responsibilities, the State operates through agencies such as An Garda Síochána, An Bord Pleanála and the Health Service Executive, which were established by legislation enacted by the Oireachtas. The administration of these powers is governed by administrative law.

The number of administrative bodies that now make decisions on behalf of the State has grown and grown. The power they wield impacts very seriously on the lives and rights of citizens. If left unchecked, this power could be open to abuse, and there is a risk that administrators may unknowingly exceed their powers and act "ultra vires". It is the function of the judiciary to protect citizens from excesses and abuses of this power, and to provide guidance to those who exercise these powers. This is done through administrative law and, in particular, through the judicial review of administrative actions.

A Note on Legal Terminology for Students

This book tries to keep the language as simple and concise as possible, avoiding legal verbosity. In particular, it tries to make as little use of legal Latin as possible. A few commonly used legal Latin phrases are: "ultra vires" (meaning "beyond powers"); "prima facie" (meaning "at first appearance"); "inter alia" (meaning "amongst other things"); and "ex parte", which refers to where one party to a case makes an application in the absence of the other party. Other than these phrases, Latin is used as sparingly as possible and is accompanied by an explanation of its meaning.

A person taking an administrative case is known as the "applicant", and the person against whom the case is taken is known as the "respondent". They are not known as "plaintiff" and "defendant", as they would be in a private law case. An affidavit is a legal document used in every judicial review, and in almost every case that goes before the courts. It is a sworn legal document and the person who swears it is called the "deponent". It contains facts that the deponent swears are true, and affidavits are usually drafted by barristers and solicitors. They are sworn in front of a commissioner for oaths or a practising solicitor. They can only contain facts the deponent knows are true, and they contain a "means of knowledge" clause which says how the deponent knows the facts are true. When reading a case title, the name of the person taking the case always goes first, so, in *Geoghegan v Institute of Chartered Accountants* [1995] 3 I.R. 86, Mr Geoghegan was the applicant taking the case against the Institute of Chartered Accountants.

2

Fair Procedures

INTRODUCTION

The fairness of procedures is of fundamental importance in administrative law. The right to fair procedures is known in Latin as "audi alteram partem", meaning "hear the other side". It is a principle of natural justice that everyone is entitled to have fair procedures applied to their case when it is being decided upon by public authorities. Fair procedures should be used in every case to prevent injustice and to ensure trust in the State and its administrative bodies. If fair procedures are not applied by an authority or decision-making body, this can be grounds for judicial review of those authorities' decisions or acts. The right to fair procedures has long been recognised: in *R. v Chancellor of the University of Cambridge* (1723) 1 Str. 557, it was said that the rule originated in the Garden of Eden. The principles of natural justice and fair procedures have their origin in common law. In *Haocher v Minister for Immigration* (1990) 169 C.L.R. 648, it was held that the precise content of the rules of natural justice vary to "reflect the common law's perception for what is necessary for procedural fairness in the circumstances of the particular case". There are two main sources which guarantee fair procedures in Irish law:

1. the Constitution; and
2. the European Convention on Human Rights (ECHR).

THE CONSTITUTION

Article 40.3.2° of the Constitution states: "The State shall, in particular, by its laws protect as best it may from unjust attack and, in the case of injustice done, vindicate the life, person, good name, and property rights of every citizen." The Supreme Court has held that fair procedures are part of the protection of the "life, person, good name and property rights of the citizen", and that the guarantee against unjust attack protects, not only against a substantively unjust attack, but also against a procedurally unjust attack. The term "constitutional justice" was first used by the Supreme Court in *McDonald v Bord na gCon* [1965] I.R. 217 when Walsh J. said that, "in the context of the Constitution natural justice might be more appropriately termed constitutional justice". In *Re Haughey* [1971] I.R. 217, the Supreme Court explained the link between constitutional justice and fair procedures. In that case, the applicant had been accused of an offence relating to funds transferred to the Irish Red Cross and had been denied the opportunity to cross-examine his accuser or to address the Dáil Public Accounts Committee in his defence. The court held that the applicant's constitutional right to fair procedures had been violated.

In *Kiely v Minister for Social Welfare* [1977] I.R. 267, Henchy J. quoted with approval the following dicta of Tucker L.J. in *Russell v Duke of Norfolk* [1949] 1 All E.R. 108:

> "There are in my view no words which are of universal application to every kind of enquiry and every kind of domestic tribunal. The requirements of natural justice must depend on the circumstances of the case, the nature of the inquiry, the rules under which [the] tribunal is acting, the subject matter that is being dealt with and so forth."

Kiely concerned the procedure for determining the level of death benefit—a widow's pension and funeral expenses—owed to a widow in her eighties. Her husband, who had been a blacksmith with Córas Iompair Éireann, had been burned in an accident at work and died four months later. Her claim for death benefit was rejected, and when she appealed this rejection, hearsay evidence—in the form of a written doctor's report—was admitted as evidence by the appeals body. Henchy J. held:

> "Natural justice is not observed if the scales of justice are tilted against one side all through the proceedings. *Audi alteram partem* means that both sides must be fairly heard. That is not done if one party is allowed to send in his evidence in writing, free from the truth-eliciting processes of a confrontation which are inherent in an oral hearing, while his opponent is compelled to run the gauntlet of oral examination and cross-examination. The dispensation of justice, in order to achieve its ends, must be even-handed in form as well as in content. Any lawyer of experience could readily recall cases where injustice would certainly have been done if a party or a witness who had committed his evidence to writing had been allowed to stay away from the hearing, and the opposing party had been confined to controverting him simply by adducing his own evidence. In such cases it would be cold comfort to the party who had been thus unjustly vanquished to be told that the tribunal's conduct was beyond review because it had acted on logically probative evidence and had not stooped to the level of spinning a coin or consulting an astrologer. Where essential facts are in controversy,

a hearing which is required to be oral and confrontational for one side but which is allowed to be based on written and, therefore, effectively unquestionable evidence on the other side has neither the semblance nor the substance of a fair hearing. It is contrary to natural justice."

In *State (Furey) v Minister for Defence* [1988] I.L.R.M. 89, McCarthy J. said that "the ... principles of natural justice as they pre-existed the constitution are now part of the human rights guaranteed by the Constitution". In *BFO v Governor of Dóchas Centre* [2005] 2 I.R. 1, Finlay-Geoghegan J. stated:

"The requirement that there be due fairness of procedures and due and proper consideration for the rights of others also appears to require that such procedures and consideration be capable of being objectively perceived to be fair. I have concluded that the procedures and decision in this instance fall short of this requirement."

In *Gallagher v Revenue Commissioners (No. 2)* [1995] 1 I.R. 55, Morris J. was of the opinion that a citizen's constitutional right to fair procedures cannot be altered or diminished by his attitude or reasons for ensuring that these rights are afforded to him. He held that rights cannot be taken away from a citizen merely because the citizen's conduct is alleged to be unmeritorious. A citizen's rights remain inviolate no matter what his motive might be for invoking the rights. In *Khan v Health Service Executive* (2010) 28 I.L.T. 73; [2009] 20 E.L.R. 178, McMahon J. noted some of the difficulties the requirement to use fair procedures may cause administrators. He said:

"To those involved in administration, adherence to fair procedure standards may appear cumbersome, irritating and even irksome on some occasions. Undoubtedly, the necessary adherence may slow down the administrators and may not be conducive to efficiency. But that is the way it is. The battle between fair procedures and efficiency has long since been fought and fair procedures have won out. The insistence on fair procedures governs all decision makers in public administration. It governs the courts as well. None of us can ignore the principle. We might wish it were otherwise. We might like to cut through procedural niceties to secure what we perceive as justice in a more expeditious way but unfortunately for decision makers that is no longer an option available to them. It is not sufficient that we justify our decision by alleging that we were focusing on the ultimate objective. It is not sufficient that we were doing our best. It is not sufficient to say that we were motivated by public health and safety objectives.

Fair procedures are at the very foundation of all legal systems and all decision makers must observe them whether we like it or not. Fair procedures are necessary for the common good."

EUROPEAN CONVENTION ON HUMAN RIGHTS

Article 6 of the ECHR states:

1. In the determination of his civil rights and obligations or of any criminal charge against him, everyone is entitled to a fair and public hearing within a reasonable time by an independent and impartial tribunal established by law. Judgment shall be pronounced publicly but the press and public may be excluded from all or part of the trial in the interest of morals, public order or national security in a democratic society, where the interests of juveniles or the protection of the private life of the parties so require, or the extent strictly necessary in the opinion of the court in special circumstances where publicity would prejudice the interests of justice.
2. Everyone charged with a criminal offence shall be presumed innocent until proved guilty according to law.
3. Everyone charged with a criminal offence has the following minimum rights:

    (a) to be informed promptly, in a language which he understands and in detail, of the nature and cause of the accusation against him;
    (b) to have adequate time and the facilities for the preparation of his defence;
    (c) to defend himself in person or through legal assistance of his own choosing or, if he has not sufficient means to pay for legal assistance, to be given it free when the interests of justice so require;
    (d) to examine or have examined witnesses against him and to obtain the attendance and examination of witnesses on his behalf under the same conditions as witnesses against him;
    (e) to have the free assistance of an interpreter if he cannot understand or speak the language used in court.

This was adopted into Irish law by s.3(1) of the European Convention on Human Rights Act 2003, which states: "Subject to any statutory provision (other than this Act) or rule of law, every organ of the State shall perform its functions in a manner compatible with the State's obligations under the Convention provisions."

Whilst not as explicit as the Irish Constitution, the ECHR also protects the right to fair procedures in civil matters as well as in criminal matters. In England, where there is no written constitution, art.6 is relied upon heavily in fair procedure cases. The scope of art.6 was extended by the European Court of Human Rights (ECtHR) in *Ringeisen v Austria* (1979–80) 1 E.H.R.R. 455, which concerned a dispute relating to land use. The ECtHR held that an administrative body—in that case, a Regional Commission—could be considered to be a tribunal under art.6.

Article 6 has subsequently been broadly interpreted. In *Delcourt v Belgium* (1979–80) 1 E.H.R.R. 355, the ECtHR held that art.6(1) should not be restrictively interpreted in the fair administration of justice. In *Transocean Marine Paint Association v EC Commission* [1974] 2 C.M.L.R. 459, the European Court of Justice held that there is a general rule of law that "persons whose interests are perceptibly affected by a decision taken by a public authority must be given the opportunity to make their point of view known".

ELEMENTS OF A FAIR HEARING

In *State (Murphy) v Kielt* [1984] I.R. 458, Barron J. held that the following were requirements of a fair hearing:

1. evidence from which it would have been fair to hold in favour of the allegation;
2. notification to the applicant of the nature of such evidence sufficient to enable him to prepare a defence;
3. time for the applicant to prepare a defence; and
4. an opportunity to make that defence.

In *Flanagan v University College Dublin* [1988] I.R. 724, Barron J. extensively discussed the right to a fair hearing and fair procedures in the context of a charge of plagiarism:

> "Clearly, the charge of plagiarism is a charge of cheating and as such the most serious academic breach of discipline possible. It is also criminal in its nature. In my view, the procedures must approach those of a court hearing. The applicant should have received in writing details of the precise charge being made and the basic facts alleged to constitute the alleged offence. She should equally have been allowed to be represented by someone of her choice, and should have been informed, in sufficient time to enable her to prepare her defence, of

such right and of any other rights given to her by the rules governing the procedure of the disciplinary tribunal. At the hearing itself, she should have been able to hear the evidence against her, to challenge that evidence on cross-examination, and to present her own evidence.

Unfortunately, there was a total failure on the part of the College to allow the applicant these rights. There was no attempt to make the applicant aware of the exact nature of the charge against her. It was not until her second telephone call to Miss Donnelly that she was made aware that it related to her choice of case history in her examination essay. Nor was she given an adequate opportunity to prepare her case or to present it. The refusal to permit her representation of her own choosing was a virtual denial of the former and the absence of anyone to give evidence against her at the hearing before the committee was a denial of one aspect of the latter. It gave her no opportunity either to discover how the case against her was being put or to test its strength by cross-examination."

THE RIGHT TO FAIR PROCEDURES

Below is a non-exhaustive list of fair procedures which should be applied in every case. It has been recognised by the courts that it is impossible to lay out exactly what can and cannot be considered fair procedures, and fair procedures should be assessed on a case-by-case basis. Certain aspects of fair procedures—for example, the rule against bias—will be dealt with separately in more detail in their own chapters.

1. the right to have notice of administrative action;
2. the right to know the case against you;
3. the right to legal representation;
4. the right to a public hearing;
5. the right to examine witnesses; and
6. the right to a prompt hearing.

THE RIGHT TO HAVE NOTICE OF ADMINISTRATIVE ACTION

Perhaps the most fundamental right to fair procedures is the right of an applicant to be told of a proposed administrative action which may adversely affect his interests. The reason for this is to allow him to make representations on the administrative action and to challenge it if necessary. This was recognised to comic effect in fiction in Douglas Adams' *The Hitchhiker's Guide to the Galaxy* (London: Pan, 1981), which begins with the protagonist's home being demolished when he was not informed of a grant of planning permission to build a bypass through it. Shortly afterwards, the Earth is demolished as the human race was not informed of plans to build a hyperspace bypass through it! In *State (Ingle) v O'Brien* [1974] 109 I.L.T.R. 7, the decision of the Garda Commissioner to revoke the licence of a taxi driver was declared invalid where no notice of intention to revoke his licence had been given to him and he had not been given an opportunity to state his case against the making of the revocation. In *Moran v Attorney General* [1976] I.R. 400, an almost identical case, the revocation of the licence was again found to be in breach of fair procedures and *audi alteram partem*. Those cases relied upon the decision in *East Donegal Co-Operative v Attorney General* [1970] I.R. 317, where the Supreme Court had to consider the constitutionality of certain sections of the Livestock Marts Act 1967. Section 3 of that Act provided for the granting, etc. of licences for livestock marts. Walsh J. held that the Minister was required:

> "... to consider every case upon its own merits, to hear what the applicant or the licensee (as the case may be) has to say, and to give the latter an opportunity to deal with whatever case may be thought to exist against the granting of a licence or for the refusal of a licence or for the attaching of conditions, or for the amendment or revocation of conditions which have already attached, as the case may be."

In *Garvey v Ireland* [1981] I.R. 75, the Commissioner of An Garda Síochána had his removal from office declared invalid because he was not given any opportunity to make representations before his removal. In *Mooney v An Post* [1998] 4 I.R. 288, Barrington J. noted that:

> "[T]he employee is entitled to the benefit of fair procedures but what these demand will depend upon the terms of his employment and circumstances surrounding his proposed dismissal. Certainly, the minimum he is entitled to is to be informed of the charge against him and to be given an opportunity to answer it and make submissions."

The Right to Know the Case Against You

Citizens have a right to know if there will be an administrative measure which will adversely affect their interests. However, this right would be worth very little if they were not given the details behind the upcoming administrative measure; consequently, applicants have a right to know the details of the case behind the administrative measure or the case against them. In *State (Murphy) v Kielt* [1984] I.R. 458, Barron J. held that the applicant was entitled to the evidence against him, as well as the evidence which was in his favour, in order to allow him to prepare a defence. In *Flanagan v University College Dublin* [1988] I.R. 724, Barron J. was of the opinion that the applicant should have received, in writing, details of the precise charge being made and the basic facts alleged to constitute the alleged offence. In *Beirne v Garda Commissioner* [1993] I.L.R.M. 1, a trainee Garda was dismissed for alleged misbehaviour on an outing. The Supreme Court held that the procedures used in his dismissal were unfair as he had not been given an appropriate opportunity to challenge specific allegations in statements made against him; and, not only was he not permitted to get mitigating evidence from the makers of the statements, he was not even shown the statements or given notice of who made them. The procedures used were unfair as he had not been given a chance to make his best case in reply to those allegations. Egan J. held:

> "The Commissioner himself did not interview the applicant and I do not suggest that he should have but certain statements taken from Garda witnesses on the bus were furnished to him. The applicant was not shown these statements and would not even appear to have been told who made them. He had no opportunity, therefore, of contradicting any specific allegations in the statements or eliciting any facts of a mitigating nature from the makers of the statements. To put it quite simply and bluntly, this was unfair."

In *O'Shea v Commissioner of An Garda Síochána* [1994] 2 I.R. 408, the applicant was not given the written account of the facts behind his dismissal. Carroll J. held:

> "In this case the applicant did not get a summary of the factual background to support the accusation against him. What he was told in the notice was the bare charge. He was entitled to the information his solicitor asked for, namely the evidence on which the allegation was based. It was not sufficient for the first respondent to say that the applicant made verbal admissions after caution ... He was entitled to a written account of the admissions he was alleged to have made and the factual background to those admissions. Since this essential requirement for natural justice was missing, the decision ... must be set aside."

Carroll J. went on to quash the order for the applicant's dismissal. A similar approach is taken in England. In *Re D (Minors) (Adoption Reports: Confidentiality)* [1996] A.C. 593, Lord Mustill stated:

FAIR PROCEDURES

"It is a first principle of fairness that each party to a judicial process shall have an opportunity to answer by evidence and argument any adverse material which the tribunal may take into account when forming its opinion. This principle is lame if the party does not know the substance of what is said against him (or her), for what he does not know he cannot answer."

In *DPP v Doyle* [1994] 2 I.R. 286, the Supreme Court noted that the Constitution guarantees fair procedures in all trials, whether summary or upon indictment. Denham J. (as she then was) found that the applicant was entitled, if it was in the interests of justice, to be provided with statements and other documents, held by the prosecution, which were being used against him in a District Court trial. In *Gallagher v Revenue Commissioners* [1991] 2 I.R. 370, Blayney J. held that where the applicant was suspended from his duties as a Customs and Excise official, natural justice required that he be given reasons for his suspension at the time, or as soon as was reasonably practicable afterwards. However, in this case the applicant knew why he was being suspended and the failure of the Revenue Commissioners to provide reasons was not a breach of natural justice. He was, however, entitled to a copy of the evidence being tendered against him in advance of his disciplinary hearing. If a court relies on material which has not been disclosed to the parties when making its decision, this will be a breach of fair procedures (*Killiney & Ballybrack Local Authority v Minister for Local Government* (1978) 112 I.L.T.R. 69).

THE RIGHT TO LEGAL REPRESENTATION

Administrative actions can be quite complex and involve issues of law about which lay people know little; as a result, a person affected by an administrative action may need to be represented by a lawyer. There is no absolute right to legal representation. However, in *State (Healy) v Donoghue* [1976] I.R. 325, the Supreme Court found that where an accused faces a serious charge and, by reason of lack of education, requires the assistance of a qualified lawyer in the preparation and conduct of a defence to the charge, then, if the accused is unable to pay for that assistance, the administration of justice requires the State to pay for it via free legal aid. In *State (Freeman) v Connellan* [1986] I.R. 433, it was held that where a court grants free legal aid, it should be very slow to refuse to assign the applicant his choice of solicitor: a court should only do so if there is good and sufficient reason. In *Bird v Judge Brady* [2008] IEHC 180, it was held that legal aid is not available in all trials of offences: if a judge is of the opinion that the imposition of a custodial sentence is unlikely, he can refuse legal aid. In *Joyce v Brady* [2011] 3 I.R. 376, it was held that the risk of imprisonment is one compelling indicator that a trial without legal aid would be unfair, but the perceived absence of such a risk is not the sole or decisive test justifying a refusal of legal aid. The absence of previous convictions, the accused's lack of familiarity with a courtroom, and the necessity of disclosure were factors in that case which should have led to the granting of legal aid.

The right to legal representation is clearly much stronger in criminal cases than in civil ones. In *Kirwan v Minister for Justice* [1994] 2 I.R. 417, the applicant had been found "guilty but insane" in respect of homicide. As a result, he was imprisoned until such time as he was adjudged not to be insane. He subsequently applied to be released on the basis that he was no longer insane, and claimed that he was entitled to free legal aid in support of his application:

> "The decision whether or not to release the applicant which the Executive is required to make is of great importance for the public and for the applicant. The interest and safety of the public is, or may be, affected by it, as is or may be, the liberty of the applicant. An applicant who is without the requisite means to procure the collection of relevant information and to formulate and present the appropriate submissions, with the information, to the committee, is necessarily, as a matter of fairness, entitled to legal aid to enable him to do so."

In *Steel and Morris v United Kingdom* (2005) 41 E.H.R.R. 22, the ECtHR held that a failure to provide legal aid to two defendants in a civil case taken against them by McDonalds infringed the right of access to a court in art.6. The ECtHR said that whether or not art.6 required legal aid in civil cases depended on "the importance of what is at stake for the applicant in the proceedings, the complexity of the relevant law and procedure, and the applicant's capacity to represent him or herself effectively". In *Flanagan v University College Dublin* [1988] I.R. 724, Barron J. was of the opinion that the applicant was entitled to be represented by a person of her choice, although, in that case, Barron J. was of the view that the case was akin to a criminal one. In *Gallagher v Revenue Commissioners* [1991] 2 I.R. 370, Blayney J. granted the applicant a declaration that he was entitled to legal representation at his disciplinary hearing. In that case, there were 72 serious charges relating to fraud against the applicant, and a police investigation had been considered. Blayney J. agreed with, and adopted the decision in, *Flanagan*. In *Corcoran v Minister for Social Welfare* [1992] I.L.R.M. 133, the applicant was a traveller who had applied for unemployment assistance. The deciding officer was suspicious of his claim as he had just bought a new van. Murphy J. held that a lay tribunal exercising a quasi-judicial function did not have to afford to the parties appearing before it an opportunity to procure legal advice or to be represented by lawyers, as the findings of the hearing were not final and could be reviewed on the basis of new evidence. In *Burns v Governor of Castlerea Prison* [2009] 3 I.R. 682, the applicants were prison officers in a disciplinary process. The relevant legislation allowed them to be represented by other prison officers but did not mention representation by lawyers. Geoghegan J. was of the opinion that the Constitution itself might require legal representation in disciplinary proceedings in exceptional cases; however, there is no need for a lawyer to be present when the issues are factual and not legal. In *Burke v O'Halloran* [2009] 3 I.R. 809, it was held that a person is entitled to refuse to be represented by a lawyer at his hearing and to instead represent himself if he so chooses.

THE RIGHT TO A PUBLIC HEARING

The right to a public hearing is protected by both Art.34.1 of the Constitution and art.6 of the ECHR. It is a long-standing legal maxim that "not only must justice be done, it must be seen to be done" (per Lord Hewitt in *R. v Sussex Justices, Ex p. McCarthy* [1924] 1 K.B. 256). Public hearings prevent abuse of power and ensure trust in the judicial process. In *Diennet v France* (1996) 21 E.H.R.R. 554, the ECtHR explained the reasoning behind this requirement:

> "The public character protects litigants against the administration of justice in secret with no public scrutiny; it is also one of the means whereby confidence in the courts can be maintained. By rendering the administration of justice transparent, publicity contributes to the achievement of the aim of Article 6(1), namely a fair trial, the guarantee of which is one of the fundamental principles of any democratic society."

The right to a public hearing has also been recognised in Ireland. Not every case will be heard in public: some cases such as rape trials or family law cases are heard in camera, meaning the public are not admitted. These exceptions are provided for under Art.34.1 of the Constitution and certain statutory provisions, including s.45 of the Courts (Supplemental Provisions) Act 1961. In prosecutions for rape, whilst the general public are not admitted, they can still be considered a public hearing as the Press are allowed attend, subject to certain restrictions. In *Barry v Medical Council* [1998] 3 I.R. 368, it was held that the Medical Council had acted in accordance with art.6 of the ECHR and had not breached the constitutional guarantee of fair procedures, when it held disciplinary proceedings for indecent assault in camera. In *Irish Times v Ireland* [1998] 1 I.R. 359, it was held that, such is the importance of public hearings, a judge cannot ban the Press from reporting on a case contemporaneously. In *Re R Ltd* [1989] I.R. 126—a company law case—

Ryanair argued that its case should be heard in camera, as it could affect its share price. It was ordered that the case be held in public. Walsh J. stated:

> "The issue before this Court touches a fundamental principle of the administration of justice in a democratic State, namely the administration of justice in public. [He then recited Art.34.1.] The actual presence of the public is never necessary but the administration of justice in public does require that the doors of the courts must be open so that members of the general public may come and see for themselves that justice is done."

The Right to Examine Witnesses

The right to cross-examine one's accusers was first recognised in *Re Haughey* [1971] I.R. 217 and was again recognised in *Flanagan v University College Dublin* [1988] I.R. 724. In *Phonographic Performances v Cody* [1998] 4 I.R. 504, Murphy J. held that "the examination of witnesses *viva voce* and in open court is of central importance in our system of justice ... it is a rule not to be departed from lightly". More recently, in *Maguire v Ardagh* [2002] 1 I.R. 385, Hardiman J. stated:

> "Where a person is accused on the basis of false statements of fact, or denied his civil or constitutional rights on the same basis, cross-examination of the perpetrators of these falsehoods is the great weapon available to him for his own vindication."

In *Kiely v Minister for Social Welfare* [1977] I.R. 267, the Supreme Court held that where one party was obliged to give evidence orally and be subject to cross-examination, and the other party could give written evidence, this was a breach of fair procedures. *Gallagher v Revenue Commissioners (No. 2)* [1995] 1 I.R. 55 concerned the judicial review of internal disciplinary proceedings brought against a Revenue Official. It was alleged that he had falsely undervalued imported second-hand cars for the purposes of vehicle registration tax. The Revenue Commissioners sought to establish the real value of the cars by the statement of witnesses from outside the jurisdiction. However, this meant that the witnesses could not be compelled to attend. Hamilton C.J. held that:

> "... depriving the ... applicant of the opportunity of challenging such evidence in cross-examination, amounted, in the particular circumstances of the case, to a deprivation of his right to fair procedures."

In *O'Broin v Ruane* [1989] I.R. 214, a District Court judge refused to allow a Garda to be cross-examined on the taking of samples in a drink driving case. It was held that this was an error within the court's jurisdiction, and therefore an appeal was a more appropriate remedy than judicial review. In *DPP v McGuinness* [1978] I.R. 189, the trial judge interrupted the cross-examination of the complainant on numerous occasions to make enquiries and remarks. The interventions were not confined to seeking clarifications of answers given by witnesses or to resolve ambiguities. The applicant's conviction was quashed and a retrial was ordered. Similar interventions occurred in the English case of *R. v Sharp* [1994] Q.B. 261, which led to the applicant's conviction being quashed.

THE RIGHT TO A PROMPT HEARING

It is a maxim of law that "Justice delayed is justice denied". The longer a person has to wait for a decision on his case, the more likely it is that he will suffer an injustice. In *McMullen v Ireland*, unreported, European Court of Human Rights, July 29, 2004, the applicant had started his case in 1988 and it had not finished by 2004. The ECtHR held that there had been a violation of his right to a trial within a reasonable time under art.6 of the ECHR. In *GE v Refugee Appeals Tribunal* [2006] 2 I.R. 11, Kearns J. noted that: "The requirement for courts of law or administrative tribunals which perform judicial-type functions to decide cases quickly is increasingly emphasised, both at international and domestic law." In *KM v Minister for Justice* [2007] IEHC 234, Edwards J. stated that "the principles of constitutional and natural justice include a right to have a decision made ... within a reasonable time". In assessing whether this right has been breached, he stated that, first, a court should address if there has been a delay in rendering the administrative decision, and secondly, if there has been a delay, whether the degree of delay is so unreasonable or unconscionable as to constitute a breach of the applicants' fundamental rights. He considered the following to be relevant in considering these issues:

1. the period in question;
2. the complexity of the issues to be considered;
3. the amount of information to be gathered and the extent of enquiries to be made;
4. the reasons advanced for the time taken; and
5. the likely prejudice to the applicant on account of the delay.

Conclusion

The right to fair procedures forms a large part of the basis of administrative law. Ultimately, the right to fair procedures can be described as the right to put forward the best possible version of one's case in a fair hearing, and the case law recognises various ways in which this can be done. The following chapters will analyse in more detail individual aspects of the right to fair procedures, such as: the rule against bias; the rules relating to errors; the requirement to give reasons; the doctrines of reasonableness and proportionality; and the doctrine of legitimate expectation.

3

Ultra Vires

INTRODUCTION

One of the most important principles of administrative law is that administrators should act within the limit of their powers. If they act outside their powers, the courts should quash these actions. The limitation of the power of authorities is one of the cornerstones of the rule of law. A key aspect of the rule of law is that all executive and administrative actions should be in accordance with law. When administrators act outside of their legal powers, they are said to be acting ultra vires. Translated from Latin, it literally means "beyond powers". Any act which is within an administrator's power is intra vires. Public bodies are often given legal powers by statute to perform certain acts which the ordinary person cannot. Limits on this power are not difficult to imagine; for example, the taxi regulator has the power to grant taxi licences but does not have the power to award a pub a drinks licence. This doctrine allows the reviewing court to determine whether or not an act or decision of a public body, lower court or administrative decision-maker is made within the limits of its power, by reference to the intention of the legislature. In *R. v Hull University Visitor Ex p. Page* [1993] A.C. 682, Lord Browne-Wilkinson explained that this doctrine formed the basis of judicial review:

> "Over the last 40 years, the courts have developed general principles of judicial review. The fundamental principle is that the courts will intervene to ensure that the powers of public decision-making bodies are exercised lawfully. In all cases, save possibly one, this intervention by way of prohibition or certiorari is based on the proposition that such powers have been conferred on the decision maker on the underlying assumption that the powers are to be exercised only within the jurisdiction conferred, in accordance with fair procedures and, in a *Wednesbury* sense, reasonably. If the decision maker exercises his powers outside the jurisdiction conferred, in a manner which is procedurally irregular or is *Wednesbury* unreasonable, he is acting *ultra vires* his powers and therefore unlawfully."

The superior courts can quash any administrative measure which is ultra vires. This is a key part of the system of checks and balances which makes up modern constitutional democracies, and is seen as being the constitutional bedrock for judicial review. *Wednesbury* unreasonableness, referred to by Lord Browne-Wilkinson above, will be analysed in Ch.6.

The ultra vires doctrine is also important in the context of company law where a company's powers may be limited by its articles of incorporation and it may not act outside those powers—see, for example, *Ashbury Railway Carriage Co v Riche* [1875] L.R. 7 H.L. 653. This is of relevance to administrative law as local authorities in Ireland have the status of a corporation.

THE ULTRA VIRES DOCTRINE IN IRELAND

The ultra vires doctrine has long been recognised in Ireland. In *Corporation of Waterford v Murphy* [1920] 2 I.R. 165, it was held that the Corporation's imposition of tolls for the use of a bridge was beyond its powers, or in excess of its jurisdiction. The Corporation was only empowered by statute to enact byelaws concerning the time and mode of boats passing through the bridge. In *Cross v Minister for Agriculture* [1941] I.R. 55, Gavin Duffy J. held that the Minister for Agriculture was acting ultra vires in defining the boundary between tidal and freshwater portions of a river when he used the limits of saline vegetable growth under the water as his criterion, rather than the statutory criterion of the limits of the tide.

When the Oireachtas enacts legislation which grants powers to persons or bodies, it will include the limit to which those powers can be exercised. When it comes to sentencing, every statute which includes an offence will include a maximum penalty for that offence. For example, the maximum penalty for threatening, abusive or insulting behaviour in a public place under s.6 of the Criminal Justice (Public Order) Act 1994 is three months' imprisonment and a fine. If a judge were to sentence a person to four months' imprisonment for this offence, he would clearly be acting beyond his powers. The jurisdictions of the Circuit and District Courts are also limited by Art.34.3.4° of the Constitution.

The definitive statement on the doctrine of ultra vires in Irish law was given by Henchy J. in *State (Lynch) v Cooney* [1982] I.R. 337:

> "I conceive the present state of evolution of administrative law in the courts on this topic to be that when a statute confers a decision-making power affecting personal rights on a non-judicial person or body, conditional on that person or body reaching a prescribed opinion or conclusion based on a subjective assessment, a person who shows that a personal right of his has been breached or is liable to be breached by a decision purporting to be made in exercise of that power

has standing to seek, and the High Court jurisdiction to give, a ruling as to whether the precondition for the valid exercise of the power has been complied with in a way that brings the decision within the express or necessarily implied range of the power conferred by the statute. It is to be presumed that when Parliament conferred the power it intended it to be exercised only in a manner that would be in conformity with the Constitution and within the limitations of the power as it is to be gathered from the statutory scheme or design. This means, amongst other things, not only that the power must be exercised in good faith, but that the opinion or other subjective conclusion set as a precondition for the valid exercise of the power must be reached by a route that does not make the exercise unlawful — such as by misinterpreting the law, or by misapplying it through taking into consideration irrelevant matters of fact, or through ignoring relevant matters. Otherwise, the exercise of the power will be held to be invalid for being *ultra vires.*"

In *McCormack v Garda Síochána Complaints Board* [1997] 2 I.R. 489, Costello P. found that an administrative decision taken in breach of the principles of constitutional justice is ultra vires:

"An administrative decision taken in breach of the principles of constitutional justice will be an *ultra vires* one and may be the subject of an order of *certiorari*. Constitutional justice imposes a constitutional duty on a decision making authority to apply fair procedures in the exercise of its statutory powers and functions. If it can be shown that that duty includes in a particular case a duty to give reasons for its decision then a failure to fulfil this duty may justify the court in quashing the decision as being *ultra vires.*"

DELEGATED LEGISLATION

Article 15.2.1° of the Constitution states: "The sole and exclusive power of making laws for the State is vested in the Oireachtas: no other legislative authority has power to make laws for the State." In practice, the Oireachtas does not have the time to legislate for every tiny detail of law. This is recognised by Art.15.2.2° of the Constitution which states: "Provision may however be made by law for the creation or recognition of subordinate legislatures and for the powers and functions of these legislatures." This was elaborated on by the Supreme Court in *City View Press v An Chomhairle Oiliúna* [1980] I.R. 381. The court held that the Oireachtas can delegate certain powers to subordinate bodies through primary legislation. This primary legislation must lay out "principles and policies" which must be obeyed by the subordinate body when it fleshes out the law. The subordinate bodies cannot create their own principles or policies but must follow those in the primary legislation. If the laws created by the subordinate body do not follow the "principles and policies", they are ultra vires. Subordinate bodies which are given these powers are most frequently Government Ministers, but they can also be other bodies.

In *City View*, the challenged statutory provisions allowed An Chomhairle Oiliúna—the industrial training authority—to impose levies on firms to finance its training activities. The legislation did not specify how those levies were to be calculated and no ceiling was imposed on the levies. However, the constitutionality of the legislation was still upheld by the Supreme Court.

Any legislation which gives a subordinate body the power to make public policy will be unconstitutional; however, the presumption of constitutionality should be noted. The presumption of constitutionality means that any legislation passed by the Oireachtas has to be interpreted in such a way as to be constitutionally valid where possible. In several cases where subordinate bodies were found to have used powers granted to them by primary legislation to make public policy, the challenged legislation was read in such a way that it would not have the effect of allowing a subordinate body to make public policy. In these cases, the primary, or parent, legislation was held to be constitutional, but the subordinate or secondary legislation—which amounted to the creation of public policy—was held to be ultra vires the primary legislation and was struck down.

In *Cooke v Walsh* [1984] I.R. 710, the Supreme Court found that regulations made by the Minister for Health providing that health services would not be available to people injured in a car crash, unless they could establish that they were not entitled to compensation or damages from a third person, were ultra vires s.72(2) of the Health Act 1970, as the legislature could not have delegated such power. Section 72(2) provided that: "Regulations made under this section may provide for any service under this Act being made available only to a particular class of persons who have eligibility for that service." In *Cooke*, the infant plaintiff had been seriously injured in a road traffic accident and would normally have been entitled to free medical care, but the regulations prevented him from receiving it. Proceeding on the principle of the presumption of constitutionality, O'Higgins C.J. felt that it was necessary to interpret the Act in a manner which rendered it constitutional. Therefore, he interpreted it as meaning that the Minister could make regulations permitting health boards not to provide certain kinds of services to persons of "limited eligibility". The Act itself was found to be constitutional, but the regulations were ultra vires.

In *Harvey v Minister for Social Welfare* [1990] 2 I.R. 232, the constitutionality of the Social Welfare Act 1952 was challenged on the grounds that s.75 empowered the Minister to make regulations which deprived the applicant of benefits he was entitled to. Similarly to *Cooke*, the court found the Act to be constitutional but the regulations were ultra vires the Minister's power. According to Finlay C.J.: "[T]he terms of s.75 do not make it necessary or inevitable that a Minister making regulations pursuant to the power therein must invade the function of the Oireachtas in a manner which would constitute a breach of the provisions of Article 15.2."

In *Leontjava and Chang v DPP* [2004] 1 I.R. 591, the applicants were foreign nationals charged with the offence of remaining within this jurisdiction beyond a date set by an immigration officer. Section 5(1) of the Aliens Act 1935 (the "1935 Act") empowered the Minister for Justice to set restrictions and conditions in respect of "aliens" landing in or entering the State, including limiting their entry to specific places. Article 5(6) of the Aliens Order 1946 (S.I. No. 395 of 1996) provided that an immigration officer could attach such conditions as the duration of an alien's stay in the jurisdiction, or conditions surrounding an alien's engagement in business in the State. The applicants sought a declaration that this article was ultra vires the Minister's power and, if necessary, a declaration that s.5(1) was unconstitutional. Keane C.J. held that there was no explicit or implicit indication in the primary legislation that the Minister's power would extend so far as to empower an immigration officer to specify a time of departure from the State; there was certainly no indication that the power would extend to an immigration officer. As a result, art.5(6) was ultra vires the Minister's power and it was therefore not necessary to examine whether or not the 1935 Act was unconstitutional. However, s.2(1) of the Immigration Act 1999 (the "1999 Act") stated that: "Every order made before the passing of this Act under section 5 of the Act of 1935 other than the orders or provisions of orders specified in the Schedule to this Act shall have statutory effect as if it were an Act of the Oireachtas." This meant that although the Aliens Order 1946 was ultra vires, the 1999 Act adopted all of the orders made under s.5 of the 1935 Act and gave them the same effect as primary legislation. This retrospective validation by the 1999 Act saved the orders and they were now constitutionally valid.

See also the cases of *Laurentiu v Minister for Justice* [1999] 4 I.R. 26 and *Mulcreevy v Minister for the Environment* [2004] 1 I.L.R.M. 419.

The Rule Against Bias

4

Introduction

One of the most important principles of administrative law is that decisions should be made by impartial administrators. It would undermine confidence in the law if administrators were biased when making their decisions. In Latin, the principle is stated as *nemo iudex in causa sua*. As Lord Hewart C.J. put it in *R. v Sussex Justices* [1924] 1 K.B. 256, "it is not merely of some importance but is of fundamental importance that justice should not only be done, but should manifestly and undoubtedly be seen to be done". Article 34.5.1° of the Constitution requires newly-appointed judges to make, and subscribe to, a declaration to exercise their power without bias. In *O'Reilly v Cassidy* [1995] 1 I.L.R.M. 311, the rule against bias was described as being "as old as the common law itself". The Supreme Court in *Dublin Wellwoman Centre Ltd v Ireland* [1995] 1 I.L.R.M. 408, adopted the Oxford English Dictionary definition of bias as being "an inclination, leaning, tendency, bent, a preponderating disposition or propensity, predisposition, predilection, prejudice". During a hearing, where there is an apprehension of bias the person concerned must make his views known to the person in charge of the hearing (*O'Reilly v Cassidy*). The principles relating to bias have been set out in the Supreme Court decision of *Orange Ltd v Director of Telecommunications Regulations (No. 2)* [2000] 4 I.R. 159. There are three forms of bias—automatic bias, subjective bias and objective bias.

Automatic Bias

Automatic bias is the least common form of bias. In automatic bias cases, the applicant merely has to prove that factors which raise an automatic presumption of bias exist. Automatic bias was originally tied to one factor—having a direct financial stake in the outcome of the case. In *Dimes v Properties of Grand Junction Canal* (1852) 3 H.L.C. 759, the then Lord Chancellor, Lord Cottenham, affirmed an order granted by the Vice-Chancellor granting relief to a company in which, unknown to the defendant and forgotten by himself, he held a substantial shareholding. It was held by Lord Campbell in the House of Lords that:

"[N]o one can suppose that Lord Cottenham could be, in the remotest degree, influenced by the interest that he had in this concern; but, my Lords, it is of the last importance that the maxim that no man is to be a judge in his own cause should be held sacred. And that is not to be confined to a case in which he is a party, but applies to a cause in which he has an interest."

In *People (Attorney General) v Singer* [1975] I.R. 408, the foreman of a jury was employed by, and had shares in, the stamp company which was alleged to have been defrauded. As a consequence, the jury's verdict was set aside. In *O'Donnell v Bank of Ireland* (*Irish Times*, September 2, 2013), Charleton J. refused an application to recuse himself on the grounds of bias. "Recuse" means to disqualify oneself from adjudicating on a matter. In that case, the applicant claimed that Charleton J. was biased as his mortgage was with Bank of Ireland. Charleton J. did not have shares in the bank or multiple morgages. He held that the claim was "frankly absurd", and that if having a bank account prevented a judge from hearing a case, nothing would get done. In *Goode Concrete v CRH Ltd* [2013] IESC 39, the trial judge owned shares in one of the parties. He made the parties aware of this and no objection was made to his hearing of the case. However, an extension of time to raise the apprehension of bias argument was granted by the Supreme Court under the unusual circumstances of this case.

Automatic bias was extended to non-financial interests in *R. v Bow Street Magistrates, Ex. p. Pinochet Ugarte (No. 2)* [2000] 1 A.C. 119. In that case, Hoffmann L.J. had heard extradition proceedings involving Augusto Pinochet, the former Chilean dictator. Hoffman L.J. was an unpaid director and chairperson of Amnesty International Charity Ltd, an organisation set up and controlled by Amnesty International. Amnesty International was given permission to act as interveners in the case. It was held that automatic bias could and should extend to cases where the judge's decision would lead to the promotion of a cause in which the judge was involved, together with one of the parties.

SUBJECTIVE BIAS

Subjective bias is also known as actual bias. Subjective bias is rarely relied upon; in the vast majority of cases where bias is raised, it will be objective bias that is raised rather than subjective bias. This is because it is easier to prove that a judge appeared to be biased than it is to prove the judge was actually biased. In *Hygeia Chemicals Ltd v Irish Medicines Board* [2010] IESC 4, it was held that subjective bias is a matter of fact to be established in the course of evidence. In *Orange Ltd v Director of Telecommunications Regulations (No. 2)* [2000] 4 I.R. 159, it was held that for subjective bias to be established, it would be necessary to prove that the administrator was deliberately setting out to mark, or hold against, a particular party, irrespective of the evidence.

OBJECTIVE BIAS

Objective bias is where there is a perception of bias rather than the presence of actual bias. In *Kenny v Trinity College* [2008] 2 I.R. 40, the Supreme Court drew from the judgment of Denham J. (as she then was) in *Bula Ltd v Tara Mines (No. 6)* [2000] 4 I.R. 412, and held that the test for deciding whether objective bias existed was:

> "... whether a reasonable person in the circumstances and with the knowledge of the facts would have a reasonable apprehension that the applicants would not have a fair hearing from an impartial judge on the issues."

The court noted that the hypothetical reasonable person would be an independent observer, who is not over sensitive, and who has knowledge of the facts. He would know both those facts which tended in favour and against the possible apprehension of a risk of bias. The court also stated that the test for objective bias did not necessarily require the relationship complained of to be between the adjudicator and a party to the case; a relationship with a witness would be enough for objective bias. The court went on to state that the Supreme Court should err on the side of caution when asked to adjudicate on whether one of its own judgments was tainted by objective bias. This test is lower than having to show that a real danger of bias exists. In *Dowling v Minister for Finance* [2013] IESC 37, the test for objective was described by the Supreme Court as being "well settled".

The Supreme Court in *O'Callaghan v Mahon* [2008] 2 I.R. 514 held that objective bias could not be inferred from legal or other errors in the decision-making process, or from a pattern of erroneous decisions. The decision in *EPI v Minister for Justice* [2009] 2 I.R. 254 discusses the principles to be applied when there is an application for a judge to recuse himself on the grounds of objective bias. The burden of proof lies with the applicant to show that there are facts which give rise to an inference of objective bias. A judge is not entitled to accept an application for recusal unless he is satisfied, on the balance of probabilities, that an objective and informed person, occupying the applicant's position, would reasonably apprehend that the respondent would not bring an impartial mind to the adjudication of the case. Below are a number of occasions where it has been found that a reasonable apprehension of bias may arise.

Prior Involvement

Administrators should have no prior involvement in disputes on which they adjudicate. Where an administrator has had an earlier involvement in the decision-making process, he should be disqualified from subsequent involvement. A good example is *Flanagan v UCD* [1988] I.R. 724. This case concerned investigations into allegations of plagarism. The matter was put to a university disciplinary committee in which the university registrar acted as prosecutor. After the student had addressed the committee, she and her representatives were asked to leave while the registrar remained with the committee. It was held that the registrar, who was convinced that the student was guilty, should not have sat with the committee while the case was being decided.

It is often the case that tribunals and administrative agencies are not entirely compliant with this requirement of fair procedures. In *Heneghan v Western Fisheries Board* [1986] I.L.R.M. 255, it was held that the prime mover in dismissal proceedings acted as "[w]itness, prosecutor, judge, jury and appeal court". In *Craig v An Bord Pleanála* [2013] IEHC 402, it was claimed that a board member was biased as he had been previously employed as a technical director of a group of consultants (or its sister company) which carried out studies in respect of the development the subject matter of the application, and he had produced what the applicant considered to be a critical and contentious report. This was rejected. In *DD v Judge Gibbons* [2006] 3 I.R. 17, it was held that the fact that an accused has appeared before the same judge on a prior occasion in relation to the same or different matters will not, of itself, give rise to an inference of bias.

Hostility

If an administrator is hostile to one of the parties, this may give rise to an apprehension of bias. In *R. (Donoghue) v Cork County Justices* [1910] 2 I.R. 271, the complainant and two of her children had been convicted of a breach of the peace. One of the magistrates was a neighbour of hers and had a long history of hostility with her family owing to the trespass of her fowl on his land. The complainant's son heard him remark after the case that he "would not leave any member of [the complainant's] family in the district". The conviction was quashed by reason of the obvious personal hostility and bias. In *State*

(Hegarty) v Winters [1956] I.R. 320, one of the parties was repeatedly told by an arbitrartor that he did not know what he was talking about, and during cross-examination, he was told that if he did not answer correctly, he would have to leave the witness box. The other side had great difficulty getting their witness to answer questions, but was not rebuked. The arbitrator's decision was quashed as a result. In *Berger v United States* 255 U.S. 22 (1921), the judge said of the defendants, who were being tried under the Espionage Act 1917, that:

> "One must have a very judicial mind indeed not to be prejudiced against the German-Americans in this country. Their hearts are reeking with disloyalty … I know a safe blower … and as between him and this defendant, I prefer the safe blower."

The defendant's convictions were reversed by the appellate court because of the judge's failure to recuse himself, despite obvious personal bias. A more recent English example is *El Faraghy v El Faraghy* [2007] EWCA Civ 1149. This was a multi-million pound divorce case involving the Saudi, Sheikh Khalid Ben Abdullah Rashid al-Fawaz. The judge made a number of jokes about his ethnic origins, including: that the sheikh could choose "to depart on his flying carpet" to escape paying costs; that he should be available to attend hearings "at this, I think, relatively fast-free time of the year", so that "every grain of sand is sifted"; and he called his evidence "a bit gelatinous … a bit like Turkish Delight". The Sheikh claimed that the judge should recuse himself as these comments showed apparent bias on the grounds of his status as a Sheikh, his Saudi nationality, his Arab ethnic origins, his Muslim faith, or some or all of those elements. The judge claimed that these statements were merely harmless jokes. The Court of Appeal found the jokes would be perceived to be racially offensive, even though that was not the intention. They were likely to cause offence and result in a perception of unfairness. The comments gave "an appearance to the fair-minded and informed observer that there was a real possibility that the judge would carry into his judgment the scorn and contempt the words convey". The judge was ordered off the case.

PRE-DETERMINATION

Where a court does not approach a matter with an open mind, but instead pre-judges the issue, this may give rise to a reasonable apprehension of bias. In *McGrath v Trustees of Maynooth College* [1979] I.L.R.M. 166, the Supreme Court distinguished between pre-determination of an issue, which is illegitimate, and a pre-disposition towards an issue, which may be legitimate. A preference which may be revised will not necessarily constitute bias, particularly when the decision has yet to be concluded. In *Hygeia Chemicals Ltd v Irish Medicines Board* [2010] IESC 4, it was held that simply saying an appeal was not likely to succeed was not enough to pre-judge the issue. Comments made by a court, or its conduct in a case, may give rise to a reasonable apprehension of pre-determination. In *P v Judge McDonagh* [2009] IEHC 316, a Circuit Court Judge made certain comments that were alleged to have pre-determined the outcome of family law proceedings, and two applications were made that he recuse himself. He refused these applications. It was held by the High Court that:

> "[I]t seems to me that there is another form of pre-judgment which arises where the adjudicator indicates that the adjudicator has reached a conclusion on a question in controversy between the parties, at a time prior to it being proper for such adjudicator to reach such a decision (indeed it might well be more accurate to describe such a situation as premature judgment rather than pre-judgment). It can hardly be said that a reasonable and objective and well informed person would be any the less concerned that a party to proceedings was not going to get a fair adjudication if, at an early stage of the hearing, comments were made by the adjudicator which made it clear that the adjudicator had reached a decision on some important point in the case at a time when no reasonable adjudicator could have, while complying with the principles of natural justice, reached such a conclusion."

Excessive interventions by a judge or tribunal can give rise to a perception that the adjudicator has "sacrificed objectivity by entering into the fray" (per Birmingham J. in *Power v Doyle* [2008] 2 I.R. 69). Similar cases include *People v McGuinness* [1978] I.R. 189 and *Dineen v Delap* [1994] 2 I.R. 228.

Family Relationship between an Administrator and a Party

O'Reilly v Cassidy [1995] 1 I.L.R.M. 311 concerned a pub licensing application and one of the barristers was the daughter of the judge hearing the case. The judge reacted angrily when he was asked to recuse himself. It was found that the mere fact that a judge's daughter appeared before him would not cause a reasonable man to consider that bias would occur; however, in the particular circumstances of this case, there was a real possibility that a reasonable person would be afraid that the outcome of the proceedings could be affected by the relationship between the judge and counsel.

The Bar Council's Code of Conduct requires barristers not to habitually practise in any court of which their parent, spouse or near blood relative is a presiding judge. When a barrister appears before a court in which his relative is a presiding judge, steps should be taken to ensure that the fact is made known to the opposing party.

PREVIOUS LAWYER/CLIENT RELATIONSHIP BETWEEN ADMINISTRATOR AND A PARTY

The leading case is *Bula Ltd v Tara Mines (No. 6)* [2000] 4 I.R. 412. In that case, the Supreme Court found that a prior relationship of legal adviser and client does not generally disqualify the former adviser from acting as an administrator in a case where his former client appears. This is because a reasonable person would know that lawyers do not develop a lifelong loyalty to the interests of their clients. A previous lawyer/client relationship between administrator and a party would only be of concern in a case where a specific piece of legal advice the lawyer had worked on became an issue in proceedings in which the lawyer was judge. The court drew from the Australian decision of *Aussie Airlines Pty Ltd v Australian Airlines* (1996) 135 A.L.R. 753, where it was held:

> "The reasonable bystander would expect that members of the judiciary will have had extensive professional associations with clients but that something more than the mere fact of association is required before concluding that the adjudicator might be influenced in his or her resolution of the particular case by reason of the association. Although the test is one of appearance it is an appearance that requires a cogent and rational link between the association and its capacity to influence the decision made in the particular case."

This approach was followed in *Keegan v Kilrane* [2011] 3 I.R. 813. In *DPP v Conmey* [2012] IECCA 75, there was an attempt by the DPP to get Hardiman J. to recuse himself from being part of an appeal court that will decide whether a man's conviction 40 years previously for manslaughter was a miscarriage of justice. The DPP unsuccessfully argued objective bias on the part of Hardiman J., arising from his being offered a brief in the case in September 1999 while still practising as a senior counsel, and also from his having been a member of the three-judge Court of Criminal Appeal that overturned the conviction in question.

POLITICAL VIEWS

Judges are political appointees. Whether or not a decision-maker's political views will disqualify him from hearing a case often depends on the closeness of connection between his political views and the case. *Dublin Wellwoman Centre v Ireland* [1995] 1 I.L.R.M. 408 concerned the right to make information about abortion available. The presiding judge had acted as the Chairwoman of the Second Commission on the Status of Women and had written to the Taoiseach stating that the Commission was of the view that women should have the constitutional right to travel abroad in order to have an abortion, and to receive counselling and information on abortion. When it came to hearing, the third-named respondent—the Society for the Protection of Unborn Children (SPUC)—requested that she discharge herself on the basis that her activities with the Commission created a reasonable apprehension of bias. The judge refused, as she was satisfied that she was not biased, and SPUC appealed this refusal. Denham J. (as she then was) held:

> "It is a fundamental and age old concept in common law that justice must manifestly and visibly be seen to be done. In cases such as this where many reasonable people in our community hold strong opinions, it is of particular importance that neither party should have any reasonable reason to apprehend bias in the Courts of Justice. Further, once the question of a possible perception of bias has been raised reasonably on grounds of pre-existing non-judicial position and actions it would be contrary to constitutional justice to proceed with a trial. I am satisfied that the learned High Court judge should have discharged herself. There is no question of a personal interest of the learned High Court judge – no subjective bias. However ... the appellant has made out the case of reasonable apprehended bias in the circumstances."

R. v Bow Street Magistrates, Ex p. Pinochet Ugarte (No. 2) [2000] 1 A.C. 119, discussed above, is also relevant in this context.

Where the objection is based on the decision-maker's general political background rather than on a specific political issue, there is a heavier burden on the objecting party. The courts will take into account two factors: first, the judicial oath to administer justice without bias; and secondly, that everyone has a level of political interest and this is natural in judicial appointees. In *President of the Republic of South Africa v SARFU* (1999) 4 SA 147 (relied upon by Denham J. (as she then was) in *Bula Ltd v Tara Mines (No. 6)*), the South African Rugby Football Union challenged the legality of an order establishing a commission of enquiry into financial and administrative matters in South African rugby. An application was made requesting four judges who, prior to appointment, had links with the ruling African National Congress party and President Mandela, to recuse themselves. It was held that the fact that a judge may have engaged in political activity prior to appointment is not uncommon in most, if not all, democracies and that it should not be a surprise. Moreover, it was held that a judge who is so remote from the world that he or she has no such views would hardly be qualified to be a judge.

Errors

5

INTRODUCTION

Administrators are only human; they can and do make mistakes which may need to be corrected. Unfortunately, the law as to when an error made by an administrator can be judicially reviewed is not entirely settled. Errors, from an administrative law point of view, can be divided broadly into three types: errors in law; errors in law on the face of the record; and errors in fact.

ERROR IN LAW

Traditionally, judicial review did not correct an error of law unless it was one which appeared on the face of the record. The leading authority for this was *R. (Martin) v Mahony* [1910] 2 I.R. 695—a judgment of all eight judges of the King's Bench Division. The avenue of appeal was instead seen as being the correct remedy where an error was made as to the law. As a result, it used to be the case that so long as a decision was made within a court's jurisdiction, it could not be impeached, even if there was no evidence to support it.

This approach was swept aside in England in the case of *Anisminic Ltd v Foreign Compensation Tribunal* [1969] 2 A.C. 147. This case arose out of the Suez Crisis and concerned compensation paid by the Egyptian Government to the British Government for properties it had seized. Lord Reid held in this case that:

> "[T]here are many cases where, although the tribunal had jurisdiction to enter on the enquiry, it has done or failed to do something in the course of the enquiry which is of such a nature that its decision is a nullity. It may have made its decision in bad faith. It may have made a decision which it had no power to make. It may have failed in the course of the enquiry to comply with the requirements of natural justice. It may in perfect good faith have misconstrued the provisions giving it power to act so that it failed to deal with the question remitted to it and decided some question which was not remitted to it. It may have refused to take into account something which it was required to take into account. Or it may have based its decision on some matter which, under the provisions setting it up, it had no right to take into account. I do not intend this list to be exhaustive."

Lord Browne-Wilkinson in *R. v Lord President of the Privy Council, Ex p. Page* [1993] A.C. 682 summed up the *Anisminic* rule as follows: "In general, any error of law made by an administrative tribunal or inferior court in reaching its decision can be quashed for error of law".

Unfortunately, it is unclear whether or not the *Anisminic* approach has been adopted by the Irish courts. In *State (Abenglen Properties) v Dublin Corp* [1984] I.R. 381, the Irish courts had an opportunity to adopt *Anisminic*, which was broadly similar in facts, but *Anisminic* was not referred to. Henchy J. in his judgment noted: "Where an inferior court or a tribunal errs within jurisdiction, without recording that error on the face of the record, certiorari does not lie"—a clear rejection of the *Anisminic* approach. The view that an appeal is a better remedy than judicial review was again reiterated in the decision in *Doyle v Judge Connellan* [2010] IEHC 287. This case involved a drug driving case where it was alleged the accused was power-sliding around a roundabout. In *Balaz v Judge Kennedy* [2009] IEHC 110, Hedigan J. said:

> "In considering the applicant's case on this ground, the Court must remain acutely aware of its function in judicial review proceedings. It is not the purpose of this unique and special remedy to empower the High Court to act as an appellate body, which may review findings of fact and critically assess in minute detail the legal principles applied by the original tribunal. In a criminal case, such as the present one, the Court has no authority to re-evaluate the evidence on its own terms. There are good reasons for the imposition of such limits on the Court's capabilities."

In *State (Holland) v Kennedy* [1977] I.R. 193, Henchy J. took a differing view:

> "I am satisfied that the error was not made within jurisdiction ... it does not necessarily follow that a court or a tribunal, vested with powers of a judicial nature, which commences a hearing within jurisdiction will be treated as continuing to act within jurisdiction. For any one of a number of reasons it may exceed jurisdiction and thereby make its decisions liable to be quashed on certiorari. For instance, it may fall into an unconstitutionality, or it may breach the requirements of natural justice, or it may fail to stay within the bounds of the jurisdiction conferred on it by statute."

In this case, Henchy J. found that the law had been interpreted erroneously and, as a result, the sentence of imprisonment was imposed without jurisdiction and the order embodying it had to be quashed. It appears from this that errors of law committed by administrative bodies and lower courts will be deemed to go to jurisdiction.

In *State (Harte) v Labour Court* [1996] 2 I.R. 171, Keane J. (as he then was) said that *Holland* was to "somewhat the same effect as *Anisminic*". The case of *DPP v Killeen* [1998] 1 I.L.R.M. 1 also appears to adopt *Anisminic*. The key dicta from *Anisminic* were cited in both cases.

In *Cork CC v Shackleton* [2011] 1 I.R. 443, Clarke J. noted that:

> "Where there has been a significant error in the interpretation of a material statutory provision leading to a decision of the property arbitrator being wrong in law, any such decision should, *prima facie* be quashed."

This approach was used in *McKernan v Employment Appeals Tribunal* [2008] IEHC 40, and it was added that a court must consider whether or not the decision of the tribunal was grounded on an erroneous view of the law and whether the decision turned on an incorrect and wrong determination of a legal issue.

The law on reviewing an error in law is at best confusing, with several contradictory judgments. It is not entirely clear whether or not the simpler English approach in *Anisminic* has been adopted into Irish law. There are several judgments which mention it obliquely or cite its key dicta. However, there are other recent judgments which prefer the older approach that so long as a decision was made within a court's jurisdiction, it cannot be impeached, even if there is no evidence to support it. This area needs clarification by the courts.

ERROR IN LAW ON THE FACE OF THE RECORD

An error in law on the face of the record occurs when there is some error on the court or administrative documents. Judicial review, and the remedy of certiorari in particular, has long been considered to be the remedy for this form of error. The difference between errors in law and errors in law on the face of the record has been abandoned in England, but as it is unclear whether or not *Anisminic* is the law in Ireland, it should be discussed here. The leading common law case on errors in law on the face of the record is *R. v Northumberland Compensation Appeal Tribunal, Ex p. Shaw* [1952] 1 All E.R. 122. This case has been cited with approval in a number of Irish cases, including *Ryan v Compensation Tribunal* [1997] 1 I.L.R.M. 194. What exactly is the record? In *Northumberland*, Lord Denning found that:

"The record must contain at least the document which initiates the proceedings; the pleadings, if any, and the adjudications; but not the evidence, nor the reasons, unless the Tribunal chooses to incorporate them. If the Tribunal does state its reasons, and those reasons are wrong in law, certiorari lies to quash the decision."

In criminal cases, the record has been held to include warrants, the transcript of the trial and formal records (see *Re Tracey*, unreported, Supreme Court, December 21, 1963). In *Bannon v Employment Appeals Tribunal* [1993] I.R. 500, the finding of Morris L.J. in the *Northumberland* case was adopted:

"It is plain that certiorari will not issue as the cloak of an appeal in disguise. It does not lie in order to bring up an order or decision for rehearing of the issue raised in the proceedings. It exists to correct errors of law which were revealed on the face of an order or decision or irregularity, or absence of, or excess of, jurisdiction where shown. The control is exercised by removing an order or decision and then quashing it."

In *Bannon*, an error of law as to the implementation of an EU directive which appeared in the Employment Appeal Tribunal's decision was held to have appeared on the record and was quashed as a result.

One important decision where a more restrictive approach was taken is *DPP v Judge O'Buachalla* [1999] 1 I.L.R.M. 362. In that case, it was contended, inter alia, that the District Court judge's conviction of the applicant for road traffic offences contained an error on the record. Quirke J. held that the District Court had jurisdiction to convict the accused and that the conviction should not be quashed on the basis of want or absence of jurisdiction. However, he found that there were what amounted to errors on the face of the record. The court found that no prejudice would be suffered by the parties involved and refused the relief sought by the applicant:

"Insofar as it has been contended on behalf of the applicant that the conviction and order is bad on its face and should be quashed on that ground, I am satisfied that the declarations contained within the order relative to the provisions of the Criminal Justice Act 1951 are erroneous and inaccurate. An explanation has been offered (although not in evidence) suggesting that the declarations resulted from clerical errors within the District Court office which, as a matter of practice, includes such declarations within orders which result from successful prosecutions made under the provisions of section 53 of the Road

Traffic Act 1961. If that explanation is accurate then it is devoutly to be hoped that this practice has now been discontinued.

Finding, as I have, that the first named respondent was endowed with jurisdiction to deal with the charge preferred against the second named Respondent and noting that the order referred to that particular charge and that the subsequent declarations are largely prolix and have no relevance to the prosecution and conviction, I am satisfied that the declarations comprised defects (if they can be described as defects) of form and not of substance and I do not believe that either of the parties to the prosecution have been in any way prejudiced by those declarations.

In particular, I do not believe that the inclusion of such declarations as are contained within the order can in any way work an injustice on any party to the proceedings and should give rise to circumstances where the second named respondent should, contrary to his wishes, be again placed in jeopardy in respect of an offence for which he has already been lawfully tried.

In the circumstances, I do not believe that it would be an appropriate exercise of my discretion to grant to the applicant the relief which he seeks on the second ground which has been advanced."

ERROR IN FACT

The general rule is that courts will not review a decision where there has been an error as to the facts. If an error in fact is made, appeal is generally seen as being a better remedy. In *Ryanair v Flynn* [2000] 3 I.R. 240, Kearns J. stated:

"The cases where the court can intervene by way of judicial review to correct errors of fact must be extremely rare ... it seems clear to me on the authorities that a very high threshold must be met, at least in this jurisdiction before the Court can or should intervene."

There is a developing line of authority relating to *material* error of fact coming from asylum-related judicial reviews. Where there is a material error of fact, the courts will be more likely to intervene. This stems from the decision of Finlay Geoghegan J. in *AMT v Refugee Appeals Tribunal* [2004] 2 I.R. 607. In that case, a Refugee Appeals Tribunal member had taken account of a fact for which she had no relevant material, and relied on that fact when finding against the applicant. Finlay Geoghegan J., in finding that this decision was invalid, said:

ERRORS

"I do not wish to suggest that every error made by a tribunal member as to the evidence given will necessarily render the decision invalid. It will, obviously, depend on the materiality of the error to the decision reached. The error must be such that the decision maker is in breach of the obligation to assess the story given by the applicant or the obligation to consider the evidence given in accordance with the principles of constitutional justice."

A good example of such a material error is *R v Refugee Appeals Tribunal* [2011] IEHC 151. This case arose from confusion as to what an applicant had said in various interviews when she was applying for refugee status. The decision in *Ryanair v Flynn* was endorsed in this case, but it was found not to apply on the facts. The mistake was not an error such as a wrong date, but was a mistake as to the asylum procedure in which the Tribunal member had been exercising jurisdiction. It is clear from this judgment that the error must be material. In *L v Refugee Appeals Tribunal* [2010] IEHC 362, the use of the title "Democratic Republic of Congo" instead of the "Republic of Congo" was found not to be a material error of fact. In *DO v Minister for Justice* [2010] IEHC 521, an error was found due to the fact that the applicant's step-father was referred to as her parent; however, Ryan J. found that this was not a "fundamental error of fact". The learned judge did not give any analysis of this test and did not comment on it, so it does not appear to be a different test or higher standard than the "material error of fact" test.

In the Supreme Court, McKechnie J. in *Donegan v Dublin City Council* [2012] IESC 18 stated that "there is jurisdiction to quash decisions on the basis that a tribunal has proceeded on an incorrect basis of fact". In support of this, he drew from the English case of *Secretary of State, Education and Science v Tameside* [1977] A.C. 1014, and a number of academic texts, rather than the asylum-related case law mentioned above. It appears, therefore, that the general rule that an error of fact cannot be judicially reviewed is being relaxed, and the courts are now more willing to intervene.

Reasons: Part 1—The Duty to Act Reasonably

6

REASONED DECISION

Administrators are given a lot of power and their decisions have a serious impact on the lives of those they affect. It is a principle of natural justice that administrators have a duty to act reasonably when making decisions which affect fundamental rights, and not to make unreasonable decisions. If an administrator makes a decision which is unreasonable, it may be quashed by judicial review, even if the decision was within its power to make. The doctrine of unreasonableness requires the court to examine the decision made, rather than the procedure followed in the making of that decision. This brings the courts close to the line between judicial review and appeal—there is a risk that the court may rehear the matter and put itself in the shoes of the decision-maker. Administrators also have a duty to give the reasons behind their decisions—this will be explored in Ch.7.

DEVELOPMENT

The development of the duty to act reasonably began with the landmark English case of *Associated Provincial Picture House Ltd v Wednesbury Corp* [1948] 1 K.B. 223. As result, the doctrine of unreasonableness is sometimes referred to as the "*Wednesbury* principles" or "*Wednesbury* unreasonableness". In *Wednesbury*, a cinema company was granted a licence by the local authority of the town of Wednesbury to operate a cinema, with the condition that no children under the age of 15 were allowed in on Sundays. Lord Greene found that although the local authority had kept within the four corners of the matters which they ought to consider, they had nevertheless come to a conclusion so unreasonable that no reasonable authority could ever have made it. He thought that the court could interfere with the decision in such a case. He held that a public authority acts unreasonably when a decision it makes is "so absurd that no sensible person could ever dream that it lay within the powers of the authority". The court gave the example of a red-haired teacher being dismissed because of her hair colour as being a decision which would be so absurd that it would be unreasonable.

The *Wednesbury* principles were restated by Lord Diplock in *Council of Civil Servants Unions v Minister for the Civil Service* [1985] A.C. 375. In that case, the applicants were challenging a decision which banned all the employees at the Government Communications Headquarters from being a member of a trade union. Lord Diplock held that *Wednesbury* unreasonableness applied to:

> "A decision which is so outrageous in its defiance of logic or of accepted moral standards that no sensible person who has applied his mind to the question to be decided could have arrived at it."

Lord Diplock's restatement of the *Wednesbury* principles was adopted into Irish law by the judgment of Henchy J. in *State (Keegan) v Stardust Compensation Tribunal* [1986] I.R. 642. The Stardust Tribunal had been set up by the Government to award compensation for personal injury and loss attributable to the Stardust disaster—a fire at the Stardust dancehall in 1981 which killed 48 people and injured hundreds more. The applicant sought to judicially review the Tribunal's refusal of his claim for damages for psychological injury which he said was caused by the deaths of two of his daughters, and the injury of a third daughter in the fire. He argued that the Tribunal ought to have decided, on the basis of the medical reports, that he was entitled to an award, and that the decision to make no award was arbitrary and capricious. When reviewing the law on reasonableness, Henchy J. said:

> "I would myself consider that the test of unreasonableness or irrationality in judicial review lies in considering whether the impugned decision plainly and unambiguously flies in the face of fundamental reason and common sense. If it does, then the decision-maker should be held to have acted ultra vires, for the necessarily implied constitutional limitation of jurisdiction in all decision-making which affects rights or duties which requires, inter alia, that the decision-maker must not flagrantly reject or disregard fundamental reason or common sense in reaching his decision."

Henchy J. linked unreasonableness to common sense and basic logic. If a decision plainly and unambiguously flies in the face of fundamental reason and common sense, it can be struck down for being unreasonable. He also indicated that where rights or duties are affected by a decision, there is a constitutional requirement that the decision must not be unreasonable.

The *Wednesbury* principles were subsequently restricted by the judgment of Finlay C.J. in *O'Keeffe v An Bord Pleanála* [1993] 1 I.R. 39. Finlay C.J. followed the decision of Henchy J. in Keegan, but stated that: "The circumstances under which the court can intervene on the basis of irrationality with the decision maker involved in an administrative function are limited and rare." He further stated:

> "[I]n order for an applicant for judicial review to satisfy a court that the decision-making authority has acted irrationally ... so that the court can intervene and quash its decision, it is necessary that the applicant should establish to the satisfaction of the court that the decision-making authority had before it no relevant material which would support its decision."

Finlay C.J. also emphasised that the court cannot interfere with the decision of an administrator merely on the grounds that: (a) it is satisfied, on the facts as found, that it would have raised different inferences and conclusions; or (b) it is satisfied that the case against the decision made by the administrator was much stronger for it. On the basis of this decision, an applicant must also prove that there was nothing before the administrator which would support the decision; this is a step further than simply proving that the decision plainly and unambiguously flies in the face of fundamental reason and common sense. *O'Keeffe* sets a high threshold in order to have a decision quashed for unreasonableness and it also shows considerable deference towards the decisions of administrators. Finlay C.J.'s judgment identified two reasons for this: (i) the legislature has assigned the questions to the administrators; and (ii) the administrators have expertise that the court does not have. In *Viridian Power Ltd v Commission for Energy Regulation* [2011] IEHC 266, Clarke J. emphasised that the assignment of responsibility by the Oireachtas to the administrator is the more important of the two factors.

As a result of the *Keegan* and *O'Keeffe* cases, the test for reasonableness in Ireland was often referred to as the "*Keegan/O'Keeffe*" test. However, there were a number of cases where the courts have not followed the stricter *O'Keeffe* elements of the test—for example *Matthews v Irish Coursing Club* [1993] 1 I.R. 346 and *Camara v Minister for Justice*, unreported, High Court, Kelly J., July 26, 2000. The test for reasonableness was re-examined in the ground-breaking decision of the Supreme Court in *Meadows v Minister for Justice* [2010] 2 I.R. 701.

The test for unreasonableness was reformulated by the Supreme Court in *Meadows v Minister for Justice* [2010] 2 I.R. 701. This case brought an element of the proportionality principle, discussed further in Ch.8, into the duty to act reasonably. In *Meadows*, the applicant was judicially reviewing the Minister for Justices's decision to deport her. She argued in the Supreme Court that the decision to make a deportation order should be quashed for unreasonableness as the Minister's decision failed to have due regard to the principle of non-*refoulement* governed by s.5 of the Refugee Act 1996. Non-*refoulement* is a principle of international law which forbids the delivery of a victim of persecution to his or her persecutor, and the applicant claimed she would be subject to female genital mutilation if returned to Nigeria. The applicant tried to challenge the adequacy of the existing test for judging unreasonableness in decision-making, and argued that the courts should submit an administrative decision which failed to protect or vindicate basic human rights to "anxious scrutiny". The "anxious scrutiny" test was one which had been used by the English courts in assessing human rights-related decisions since *R. v Secretary of State for the Home Department, Ex p. Bugdaycay* [1987] A.C. 514. The Supreme Court did not adopt the "anxious scrutiny" test but instead found that the test in *Keegan* is the appropriate test for determining unreasonableness, and further found that it had always incorporated the principle of proportionality. Murray C.J. stated:

> "In examining whether a decision properly flows from the premises on which it is based and whether it might be considered at variance with reason and common sense I see no reason why the Court should not have recourse to the principle of proportionality in determining those issues. It is already well established that the Court may do so when considering whether the Oireachtas has exceeded its constitutional powers in the enactment of legislation. Application of the principle of proportionality is in my view a means of examining whether the decision meets the test of reasonableness. I do not find anything in the dicta of the Court in *Keegan* or *O'Keeffe* which would exclude the Court from applying the principle of proportionality in cases where it could be considered to be relevant. Indeed in *Fajujonu v. Minister for Justice* [1992] IR 151 ... this Court made express reference to the need of the Minister to observe the principle of proportionality. In *Radio Limerick One Limited v. I.R.T.C.* [1997] 2 ILRM 1., Keane J, with whom other members of the Court concurred, acknowledged, if to a qualified extent, that the principle of proportionality may have a role to play in examining

whether an administrative decision could be considered to be invalid on the grounds of irrationality."

Denham J. (as she then was) said:

"Where fundamental rights and freedoms are factors in a review, they are relevant in analysing the reasonableness of a decision. This is inherent in the test of whether a decision is reasonable. While the test of reasonableness as described in *Keegan* and in *O'Keeffe* did not expressly refer to a concept of proportionality, and while the term "proportionality" is relatively new in this jurisdiction, it is inherent in any analysis of the reasonableness of a decision."

Denham J. was drawing from the decision of Keane J. (as he then was) in *Radio Limerick One Ltd v Independent Radio and Television* [1997] 2 I.R. 291, where he found that the measure impugned "would clearly be a reaction so disproportionate as to justify the court in setting it aside on the ground of manifest unreasonableness". She went on to find that in order for a decision which interferes with constitutional rights to be considered reasonable, it should be proportionate. She then stated:

"I am satisfied that the test in *[Keegan]* should be applied, and in construing whether the decision was reasonable it is part of that analysis to determine whether it was within the implied constitutional limitation of jurisdiction which affects rights, whether the decision was proportionate."

Fennelly J. agreed with both Denham J. and Murray C.J. This meant that when a court determines whether or not a decision was reasonable, it must take into account whether or not the decision, when it was being made, was examined for proportionality. Lack of proportionality in a decision was not defined as a new or separate ground of illegality. It was identified as one of the factors which may make a decision illegal where it impacts upon the constitutional or fundamental rights of the persons to whom the decision is addressed. It is also clear from the judgment in *Meadows* that the *Keegan* approach is preferred over the *O'Keeffe* approach and that the burden of proof lies with the applicant to satisfy the court that the decision was unreasonable. *Meadows* is a very important case, and its impact on administrative law has been assessed by a number of High Court decisions.

In *Efe v Minister for Justice* [2011] 2 I.R. 798, Hogan J. reviewed what was the appropriate test for determining reasonableness and rationality. He found that:

"It is clear that, post *Meadows* ... it can no longer be said that the courts are constrained to apply some artificially restricted test for review of administrative decisions affecting fundamental rights on reasonableness and rationality grounds. This test is broad enough to ensure that the substance and essence of constitutional rights will always be protected against unfair attack, if necessary through the application of a *Meadows* style proportionality analysis."

It appears from Hogan J.'s analysis that the effect of *Meadows* may not be as modest as the Supreme Court had seemed anxious to suggest. In *S(O) v Minister for Justice* [2010] IEHC 343, Cooke J. stated:

"The significance of the *Meadows* judgment lies not in any alteration of the *O'Keeffe* test of unreasonableness in favour of the so called 'anxious scrutiny test' - which the Supreme Court explicitly rejects - but in the clarification that the principle of proportionality is applicable as a facet of that test. The lack of proportionality in a decision is not defined as a new or separate ground of illegality. It is identified as one of the factors which may render a decision illegal as unreasonable in the sense of the pre-existing law where the decision under examination bears upon the constitutional or fundamental rights of the persons to whom the decision is addressed."

These judgments lead to the question of how an examination of proportionality should be established—should the court make its own decision as to what was proportionate and then decide that the decision-maker's decision was unreasonable? Or should a court make sure the decision-maker took account of all considerations and made a decision on proportionality which was not unreasonable? A number of cases take the view that the second approach is the correct one. The court should ensure that the process was fair and that the conclusion of the administrator that the decision was proportionate was not unreasonable. In *F (ISO) (a Minor) v Minister for Justice* [2010] IEHC 386, Cooke J. explained that:

"The High Court is not entitled or obliged to re-examine the case with a view to deciding whether, in its own view, the correct balance has been struck. To do so would be to substitute its own appraisal of the facts, representations and circumstances for that of the Minister. As the Supreme Court made fully clear in the *Meadows* case, the test to be applied in assessing whether an administrative decision of this nature is irrational or unreasonable (including unreasonable by virtue of disproportionality), remains that established in the *Keegan* and

O'Keeffe cases. Accordingly, the function of the Court is to consider the manner in which the evaluation has been made by the Minister ... and ask itself in paraphrase of the terms formulated by Henchy J: 'Does the conclusion to deport the applicant flow from the premise upon which it is based; or does it, by reason of some flaw or failure in the way in which the balancing exercise was apparently approached, result in a conclusion which "plainly and unambiguously flies in the face of fundamental reason and common sense?"'"

In *OA v Minister for Justice* [2011] IEHC 78, Clark J. felt she had to examine whether it was "unreasonable and therefore disproportionate" to expect a mother and her children to move to Nigeria to enjoy family life with their father. Clark J. felt that the conclusion that a decision was proportionate follows automatically from the conclusion that the Minister for Justice followed the correct process in the case:

"If ... having fully considered all relevant submissions made to him, the Minister makes the deportation order because he is satisfied that family life can reasonably be continued with the deported parent in the receiving country, then the reason for the deportation will be proportionate to the Minister's legitimate objective of immigration control."

However, Clark J. was also of the opinion that *Meadows* was not a particularly significant decision, as she added in her judgment that: "Clearly the inclusion of proportionality as part of reasonableness did not have its origins in *Meadows.*" So this case is perhaps of less help when assessing how *Meadows* is to be interpreted than those cases decided by Cooke J.

It is clear that *Meadows* has not been extended or given broader meaning by these decisions. Instead, they have restricted it.

GROWING UNHAPPINESS WITH THE DUTY TO ACT REASONABLY IN OTHER COMMON LAW JURISDICTIONS

The duty to act reasonably is becoming increasingly unpopular in other common law jurisdictions. In England and Wales, the view is increasingly being expressed that the *Wednesbury* test is not an adequate protection of human rights—see *R. v Ministry of Defence, Ex p. Smith* [1996] Q.B. 517; *R. v Lord Saville, Ex p. A* [2000] 1 W.L.R. 1855; and *R. (Daly) v Home Secretary* [2001] 2 W.L.R. 1622. In *Daly*, Lord Steyn explained the difference between the proportionality principle and unreasonableness as follows:

"First, the doctrine of proportionality may require the reviewing court to assess the balance which the decision maker has struck, not merely whether it is within the range of rational or reasonable decisions. Secondly, the proportionality test may go further than the traditional grounds of review inasmuch as it may require attention to be directed to the relative weight accorded to interests and considerations."

It has also come under fire in Canada. In *Dunsmuir v New Brunswick* (2008) 291 D.L.R. (4th) 577, a legal officer was dismissed for poor job performance. This case ultimately saw the Canadian Supreme Court move from three standards—correctness, reasonableness simpliciter, and patent unreasonableness—in favour of a two-tier test of correctness and reasonableness.

CONCLUSION

It is clear from the case law that administrative decision-makers have a duty to act reasonably when making their decisions. If an applicant for judicial review feels the decision taken was unreasonable, the burden of proof to show that it was lies with the applicant. It appears that the *Keegan* decision is the preferred method of assessing what is unreasonable—an unreasonable decision is one which plainly and unambiguously flies in the face of fundamental reason and common sense. However, the *O'Keeffe* dicta—that the decision-maker had before it no relevant material which would support its decision—still remains good law. Since *Meadows*, the courts, when assessing whether a decision-maker acted reasonably, can look and see if an evaluation of proportionality was made, and if it was not, then this is another factor which can be taken into account when deciding if a decision was unreasonable.

Reasons: Part 2—The Duty to Give Reasons

7

REASONED DECISION

Not only is an applicant entitled to a reasonable decision, as discussed in the previous chapter, but he is also entitled to the reasons why the administrator came to its decision. Reasons are necessary to make effective a person's right to seek judicial review. Without the reasons, a person may not be able to tell whether or not he has grounds to appeal or judicially review a decision successfully. A bad decision could be protected by simply not giving the reasons for it; a person whose rights are affected would be in the dark as to why the decision was made and he will have a hard time proving his case without the reasons for the decision. If decision-makers have to give the reasons for their decisions, they will take more care in making them as they may have to stand over the reasons in future and cannot rely on flimsy or unrealistic reasons when coming to their decisions.

Traditionally, decision-makers were not required by the common law to give the reasons behind their decisions. It was always seen as desirable that they provide reasons but they were not obliged to, and their decisions could not be reviewed if reasons were not given (*Kiely v Minister for Social Welfare* [1977] I.R. 267). For example, in *Crossan v King's Inns* [1999] IEHC 80, the applicant challenged a refusal of the King's Inns to defer examinations. It was held by Smyth J. that:

> "The fact that reasons might have been desirable is not *ad rem*, (to the point) they were neither mandatory or warranted in the circumstances ... I am satisfied on a consideration of *Rajah v The College of Surgeons* [1994] 1 IR 384 that a decision such as the Respondent's decision in the instant case was not of a nature that necessitated the giving of reasons."

It was felt that if reasons were given, then they would be over-analysed in order to find any potential grounds of appeal, which would draw out matters by leading to further litigation, thereby creating an administrative and financial burden. However, there has been a shift in judicial attitudes and the right to a reasoned decision is now recognised as part of the overarching principle that fair procedures must be applied when administrative decisions are made.

This development has come from two sources:

1. constitutional justice; and
2. legislation.

CONSTITUTIONAL JUSTICE

Throughout the 1980s and 1990s, the right to reasons was recognised and developed by the courts as a part of the constitutional right to fair procedures. In *State (Creedon) v Criminal Injuries Compensation Tribunal* [1989] I.L.R.M. 104, the applicant's husband had been killed whilst trying to stop a van, containing their child, from rolling down a hill onto a road where other children were likely to be playing. The compensation scheme provided compensation to the dependants of someone who died in the course of attempting to save a life, but the applicant's claim was denied. Finlay C.J. was critical of the Tribunal's failure to give reasons when denying the applicant's claim, saying:

> "... for a tribunal of this nature, even though it is not of statutory origin and is set up by an administrative decision by the Government, to reach a conclusion rejecting in full the claim of an applicant before it and not to give any reason for that rejection is not an acceptable and proper form of procedure ... to reject the application and when that rejection was challenged subsequently to maintain a silence as to the reason for it, does not appear to be consistent with the proper administration of functions which are of a quasi-judicial nature."

In *State (Daly) v Minister for Agriculture* [1987] I.R. 165, it was held that the Minister was obliged to give the reasons for his decision to dismiss a civil servant once his decision was challenged. In *International Fishing Vessels v Minister for the Marine (No. 1)* [1989] I.R. 149, judicial review was sought when the Minister failed to give reasons "as a matter of policy" for the refusal of a licence. Blayney J. held that when the Minister was making his decision to award licences, he was obliged to act fairly and judicially in accordance with the principles of constitutional justice, and that this obligation involved a duty to give the reasons for his decision. Unless the Minister gave his reasons, it could not be said that the procedure he adopted was fair. Blayney J. reasoned as follows:

"It is common case that the Minister's decision is reviewable by the court. Accordingly, the applicant has the right to have it reviewed. But in refusing to give his reasons for his decision the Minister places a serious obstacle in the way of the exercise of that right. He deprives the applicant of the material it needs in order to be able to form a view as to whether grounds exist on which the Minister's decision might be quashed. As a result, the applicant is at a great disadvantage, firstly, in reaching a decision as to whether to challenge the Minister's decision or not, and secondly, if he does decide to challenge it, in actually doing so, since the absence of reasons would make it very much more difficult to succeed. A procedure which places an applicant at such a disadvantage could not in my opinion be termed a fair procedure, particularly where the decision which the applicant wishes to challenge is of such crucial importance to the applicant in its business."

In *Dunnes Stores v Maloney* [1999] 3 I.R. 542, Laffoy J. held that applicants were "entitled to explore the possibility of obtaining redress by way of judicial review … In the absence of reasons, they cannot explore the possibility of or pursue redress by way of judicial review". In Laffoy J.'s opinion, procedural fairness required that the Minister give the reasons for her decision, as the applicants had demonstrated that they believed bona fide that the Minister had misused her power. Regardless of whether or not that belief was well-founded, the applicants were entitled to explore the possibility of obtaining redress by way of judicial review.

In *Rajah v Royal College of Surgeons* [1994] 1 I.R. 384, Keane J. (as he then was) said:

"In general, bodies which are not courts but which exercise functions of a judicial or *quasi* judicial nature determining legal rights and obligations must give reasons for their decisions, because of the requirements of constitutional and natural justice and in order to ensure that the superior courts may exercise their jurisdiction to enquire into and, if necessary, correct such decisions … The requirement to give reasons may extend even further to purely administrative bodies, at least where their decisions affect legal rights and obligations."

However, he found, on the facts, that the decision to dismiss a student from the Royal College of Surgeons was not one which necessitated the giving of reasons.

A restrictive approach was taken by the High Court in *McCormack v Garda Síochána Complaints Board* [1997] 2 I.R. 489. This case concerned allegations that a Garda had extracted incriminating statements from the applicant under duress. It was further alleged that the Garda had visited the applicant in Wheatfield prison and warned him against pursuing an appeal. Costello P. rejected the argument that there was a general duty to state reasons for all public decisions. He noted that the decision in *International Fishing Vessels Ltd* held that the refusal to give reasons deprives the applicant of the ability to form a view on whether or not grounds exist on which a decision might be reviewed, which places an applicant at a disadvantage. He also noted that procedures which produced such a result were constitutionally unfair. However, he proceeded to hold, somewhat contradictorily, that a person aggrieved by a decision has no right to obtain reasons for it merely for the purpose of seeing whether or not the decision-maker had erred, and said that he did not think that *International Fishing Vessels Ltd* should be so construed. He held:

> "It is not the law of this country that procedural fairness requires that in every case an administrative decision-making authority must give reasons for its decisions. Where a claim is made that a breach of a constitutional duty to apply fair procedures has occurred by a failure to state reasons for an administrative decision the court will be required to consider (a) the nature of the statutory function which the decision-maker is carrying out, (b) the statutory framework in which it is to be found and (c) the possible detriment the complainant may suffer arising from the failure to state reasons."

In Costello P.'s opinion, the issue could be determined by considering whether some detriment is suffered by an applicant through the failure to give reasons. If no detriment is suffered, then, in his opinion, no unfairness can be said to exist. This test was used by Kelly J. in *Flood v Garda Síochána Complaints Board* [1997] 3 I.R. 321, where he also found that the Board was not required to give reasons.

In *Orange Communications Ltd v Director of Telecommunications Regulations (No. 2)* [2000] 4 I.R. 159, Barron J. said that, "quite clearly the right to be given reasons for a decision springs from the guarantee of fair procedures and the obligation upon those vested with statutory powers to exercise them fairly". In *McGeown v Judge Coughlan*, unreported, High Court, Peart J., ex tempore, July 11, 2005, the applicant was accused of drink driving. At the end of the prosecution's case, he sought a direction of no case to answer. The respondent District Court judge refused this but did not provide any reasons, simply stating that the applicant was "as pissed as a monkey". The High Court quashed this decision and held that no citizen should be subject to such treatment when appearing before a court.

In *Clare v Kenny* [2009] 1 I.R. 22, MacMenamin J. stated:

"... a court in judicial review proceedings cannot act on what must be at best a hypothesis as to the possible rationale for the decision, particularly so in the context of the array of possible reasons, some of which would go beyond jurisdiction ... The situation required a decision so that all the parties would be aware precisely of their positions. The reason or rationale for the decision as to jurisdiction unfortunately cannot be inferred from what was said by the respondent."

In *Meadows v Minister for Justice, Equality and Law Reform* [2010] 2 I.R. 701, Murray C.J. stated:

"An administrative decision affecting the rights and obligations of persons should at least disclose the essential rationale on foot of which the decision is taken. That rationale should be patent from the terms of the decision or capable of being inferred from its terms and its context. Unless that is so then the constitutional right of access to the Courts to have the legality of an administrative decision judicially reviewed could be rendered either pointless or so circumscribed as to be unacceptably ineffective."

There have been some recent Supreme Court developments in this area. In *Rawson v Minister for Defence* [2012] IESC 26, an airman was dismissed from the Defence Forces after a positive random drugs test. He denied that he had taken drugs; his case was that he had been exposed to the cannabis smoke of his friends in a car. The drug testing regulations did not allow a person to be dismissed from the Defence Forces if a reasonable doubt existed as to his deliberate taking of drugs. The recommendation of the General Officer Commanding simply stated that he was to be dismissed from the Defence Forces and gave no further details. The decision of the appeals board was to the effect that his appeal against dismissal was rejected and that his discharge was to proceed. In the Supreme Court, Clarke J. concluded that if a person affected by a decision did not have sufficient information from the terms of the decision as to whether the correct question had been addressed, then it followed that the person's constitutional right of access to the courts to have the decision judicially reviewed was likely to be, in the words of Murray C.J. in *Meadows*, "rendered either pointless or so circumscribed as to be unacceptably ineffective". The decision was quashed as it did not, on its face, disclose that the decision-maker considered the question of whether a reasonable doubt had been raised. As Clarke J. put it:

"The problem in this case is that the court does not even know that the decision maker asked himself any of those questions for we know nothing about the basis of the decision to discharge Airman Rawson except that it was made and that the materials before the decision maker included Airman Rawson's representations. In my view that is insufficient to meet the requirement that the court be able to be satisfied, in the event of a challenge, that the decision maker asked the right question."

The most recent Supreme Court decision on the extent to which decision-makers are obliged to give reasons is *Mallak v Minister for Justice* [2012] IESC 59. In that case, the Supreme Court gave a detailed analysis of the principles behind the duty to give reasons. It was held that it was not possible for the appellant, without knowing the Minister's reason for refusal of a certificate of naturalisation, to ascertain whether he had a ground for applying for judicial review, and, as a result, it was not possible for the courts to effectively exercise their power of judicial review. Fennelly J. held:

"In the present state of evolution of our law, it is not easy to conceive of a decision-maker being dispensed from giving an explanation either of the decision or of the decision-making process at some stage. The most obvious means of achieving fairness is for reasons to accompany the decision. However, it is not a matter of complying with a formal rule: the underlying objective is the attainment of fairness in the process. If the process is fair, open and transparent and the affected person has been enabled to respond to the concerns of the decision-maker, there may be situations where the reasons for the decision are obvious and that effective judicial review is not precluded."

He added:

"The developing jurisprudence of our own courts provides compelling evidence that, at this point, it must be unusual for a decision maker to be permitted to refuse to give reasons. The reason is obvious. In the absence of any reasons, it is simply not possible for the applicant to make a judgment as to whether he has a ground for applying for a judicial review of the substance of the decision and, for the same reason, for the court to exercise its power. At the very least, the decision maker must be able to justify the refusal."

It is clear that this approach is much more liberal than the decision of Costello P. in *McCormack*. The requirement that decision-makers provide decisions is much heavier. The only situations now where they are not required to provide reasons for a decision is if the reasons for that decision are obvious; otherwise, the default position appears to be that reasons must be given.

LEGISLATIVE SOURCES

FREEDOM OF INFORMATION ACT 1997

The main legislative source of the right to reasons is the Freedom of Information Act 1997. Section 18 creates a statutory duty on public bodies to provide reasons for acts to the persons affected by those acts. The definition of an "act" includes a decision. Section 18(1) provides:

> The head of a public body shall, on application to him or her in that behalf, in writing or in such other form as may be determined, by a person who is affected by an act of that body and has a material interest in a matter affected by the act to which it relates, not later than 4 weeks after receipt of the application, cause a statement in writing or in such other form as may be determined to be given to the person—
> (a) of the reasons for the act, and
> (b) of any findings on any material issues of fact made for the purposes of the act.

"Public body" is very widely defined by the Act. It includes:

- all Government Departments;
- approximately 60 Government agencies, including An Bord Pleanála, the Defence Forces and the office of the DPP;
- local authorities;
- the Health Service Executive; and
- bodies prescribed by Government regulations, such as An Garda Síochána.

The definition is far-reaching and almost anything that can be seen as a public body falls within it. Section 18(2) exempts certain records from freedom of information requests. In practice, the most common of these exempted records is the decision of the Minister for Justice not to grant citizenship (see *Jiad v Minister for Justice* [2010] IEHC 187 and *Abuissa v Minister for Justice* [2010] IEHC 366). Decisions made by courts, tribunals and the President are also exempted (see s.46 of the Act for a complete list of those who are exempted).

The freedom of information procedure is simple—any person who has a material interest affected by an act of a public body may apply to the head of the body to be given the reasons for the act. The requestor must show that his request for access is made pursuant to a right of access (*Deely v Information Commissioner* [2001] 3 I.R. 439). The head of the body is required to give the reasons in writing not later than four weeks following the receipt of the application. There is no fee for a freedom of information application under s.18.

Findings on any material issues of fact, which an applicant is entitled to under s.18(1)(b), refer to matters taken into account by the decision-makers in making the decision. According to *Killilea v Information Commissioner* [2003] 8 I.C.L.M.D. 9, these matters may include:

(1) all the steps of reasoning linking the facts to the ultimate decision;
(2) the criteria relevant to the decision, the weighting attached to each criterion and the conclusion reached on each;
(3) any internal rules and guidelines used as part of the decision-making process;
(4) details of any recommendations, reports or investigations carried out by subordinate officers or experts and considered in the decision-making process.

OTHER LEGISLATION

Certain areas of law are frequently judicially reviewed. These areas have specialised provisions covering judicial review and the obligation to provide reasons.

The decision to grant planning permission in planning law is currently governed by s.34(10)(a) of the Planning and Development Act 2000, which states: "A decision ... shall state the main reasons and considerations on which the decision is based ... ."

The decision to make a deportation order in immigration law is governed by s.3(3)(a) of the Immigration Act 1999. This requires the Minister, when proposing to make a deportation order, to notify the person concerned of the proposal and the reasons for it.

LEVEL OF DETAIL NEEDED WHEN GIVING REASONS

In *O'Donoghue v An Bord Pleanála* [1991] I.L.R.M. 750, Murphy J. said:

"It is clear that the reason furnished by the Board (or any other tribunal) must be sufficient first to enable the courts to review and secondly to satisfy the persons having recourse to the tribunal that it has directed its mind adequately to the issue before it. It has never been suggested that an administrative body is bound to provide a discursive judgment as a result of its deliberations."

The Supreme Court considered the level of detail which must be given when giving reasons in *FP v Minister for Justice* [2002] 1 I.R. 164. It agreed that, when providing reasons, administrative bodies have never been bound to provide a discursive judgment as a result of its deliberations. It also held that the degree to which a decision must be supported by reasons, stated in detail, will vary with the nature of the decision itself. In a case where there are several possible reasons, some capable of being unknown, even in their general nature, to the person affected, then a more ample statement of reasons is required than in simpler cases where the issues are more defined.

In *Sisk v District Judge O'Neill* [2010] IEHC 96, the President of the High Court rejected a challenge to the decision of District Judge O'Neill. This was a drink driving case and at the end of the prosecution case, counsel for the applicant had made detailed submissions on the illegality of the applicant's detention on the side of the road and the unfairness of procedure where the Garda instruction manual on breath specimens had not been complied with. In response to these submissions, the judge said: "I am not going to grant a direction. I do want to hear your client." Kearns P. felt it was not necessary for the judge to have offered any legal rationale for this ruling. This case is currently under appeal to the Supreme Court.

In *Mulholland v An Bord Pleanála (No. 2)* [2006] 1 I.R. 458, it was held that the reasons must enable the person affected by the decision to know if the decision-maker had adequately directed his mind to the issues; the reasons must give a person sufficient information to enable him to consider whether he would have a reasonable chance of succeeding in appealing or judicially reviewing the decision; and the reasons must be sufficient to enable the High Court to review the decision.

Murray C.J. pointed out in *Meadows* that a right of judicial review is rendered pointless unless the party has access to sufficient information to enable it to assess whether the decision sought to be reviewed is lawful, and to enable the courts, in the event of a challenge, to have sufficient information to determine that lawfulness. This was followed by Clarke J. in *Rawson*, who added that in some cases, the material on which a challenge might be considered may be obvious.

Are Judges Required to Give Reasons?

The judiciary are not obliged to give reasons by the Freedom of Information Act 1997 or any of the other statutes mentioned above. However, Art.34.1 of the Constitution requires that they operate in accordance with justice. It is difficult to see why they should not be obliged to provide reasons for their decisions when administrative bodies are, particularly given their legal experience and training. This issue was addressed in *Foley v Murphy* [2008] 1 I.R. 619, which reviews the law in Ireland, England and at a European level. McCarthy J. found a decision to refuse costs to a successful defendant should have been more explicitly spelt out. The applicant could not know whether or not he had a good ground on which to seek judicial review, either on the basis of an error of law or that the decision was irrational or unreasonable. As a result, the decision was a nullity as a breach of the constitutional entitlement to fair procedures. It is now clear that judges have a duty to provide the reasons for their decisions. Clarke J. noted in *Rawson* that "it has consistently been held that parties who have a right of appeal within a process are entitled to sufficient information to enable them to consider, and if appropriate to mount, such an appeal". As there is an automatic right of appeal from the District Court, it would imply this duty lies most heavily on District Court judges.

Conclusion

In conclusion, it can be said that a citizen who is the subject of a decision has a right to the reasons behind that decision. If the reasons for that decision are already clear, then they may not be entitled to them. The reasons do not have to be overly detailed, but they should be detailed enough to let the citizen know whether or not the decision could be successfully judicially reviewed. In cases where there is a right of appeal, this duty is even more important.

The Doctrine of Proportionality

8

INTRODUCTION

Proportionality is a legal principle which had its origins in German law, but which has since spread to the other EU Member States. It requires that there be a balance between the public interest achieved by an administrative action which affects someone's rights and the adverse effects which are caused by the action. Administrative measures must not be arbitrary, unfair or based on irrational considerations. For example, if the Government was worried about littering, and introduced a mandatory life sentence for anyone caught littering, this would clearly be disproportionate, as the measure goes far in excess of what is needed to tackle the problem. A good example of a disproportionate measure can be seen in *R. v Barnsley M.B.C., Ex. p Hook* [1976] 1 W.L.R. 1052. In that case, a street trader was banned for life from trading in a market when he was caught urinating nearby. The sanction was quashed as there was a lack of proportionality between the applicant's action and the administrative measure which deprived him of his livelihood, particularly as the lesser measure of a fine was available. The proportionality principle is of increased importance in Ireland due to the Supreme Court decision in *Meadows v Minister for Justice, Equality and Law Reform* [2010] 2 I.R. 701, which tied the proportionality principle in with the duty to act reasonably. This case is discussed in more detail in Ch.6. Unfortunately, the exact position of the proportionality doctrine in Ireland is still unclear. According to O'Donnell J. in *Nottinghamshire CC v KB* [2011] IESC 48:

> "It has now become common place to refer to proportionality in constitutional litigation. I think it is necessary however to recognise that proportionality in itself is not an entirely transparent concept. It can be applied strictly to strike down legislation or generously to sustain it. It is important to remember that proportionality is a tool for analysis, rather than an end in itself. The mere statement that something is *proportionate* is almost as delphic as the statement that it is *reasonable*. The analysis of whether any particular restriction or limitation is consistent [with] the Constitution may be assisted by the structure [that a] proportionality analysis provides, but only if it is

explained *why* any particular provision is permitted by the Constitution, and is proportionate. In my view it is an error to approach the constitutional issue by simply asking, almost in the abstract, whether any particular provision is proportionate as an almost self standing test of constitutionality and detached from careful consideration of the text and the values necessarily implied by it."

O'Donnell J. was speaking of challenges to legislation rather than administrative actions, and the case in question did not involve a challenge to legislation (it involved the interpretation of art.20 of the "Brussels II" regulation). However, the issue of proportionality translates between the different areas of law.

PROPORTIONALITY TEST

The use of the proportionality test as a basis for challenging legislation is well-established in Irish law. It was first considered in *Hand v Dublin Corp* [1989] I.R. 26, and first used in *Cox v Ireland* [1992] 2 I.R. 503. In that case, the Supreme Court struck down provisions of the Offences against the State Act 1939 as being a disproportionate violation of, inter alia, the plaintiff's property rights and right to earn a livelihood. In *Heaney v Ireland* [1994] 3 I.R. 593, the High Court set out a three-part test for assessing the proportionality of a measure. In order for a measure to be proportionate, it must:

(a) be rationally connected to the objective and not be arbitrary, unfair or based on irrational considerations;
(b) impair the right as little as possible; and
(c) be such that its effects on rights are proportional to the objective.

The so-called *Heaney* test was approved by the Supreme Court in *Rock v Ireland* [1997] 3 I.R. 484. In *Holland v Governor of Portlaoise Prison* [2004] 2 I.R. 573, a blanket policy on communication with the media was successfully challenged by a prisoner on the grounds that it was disproportionate. McKechnie J., in applying the *Heaney* test, held that:

"I do not believe that the respondent has satisfied this court as to a necessity for such a blanket ban which, in my view, is entirely disproportionate to the penal objective which he seeks to maintain. This objective is one which I think is properly legitimate but, it is the means adopted to achieve its results which, in my view, are unlawful. Therefore, I remain of the opinion that this ban cannot be justified."

In the recent case of *Meadows v Minister for Justice, Equality and Law Reform* [2010] 2 I.R. 701, proportionality was endorsed by Denham J. (as she then was) in the Supreme Court, who noted that it was "relatively new in this jurisdiction" and that it had its origins in the civil law countries of Europe. In *Meadows*, the judges of the Supreme Court expressly stated that proportionality can be used as a means of challenging administrative actions that infringe fundamental rights. Unfortunately, they differed over what exact test should be used in assessing proportionality, and did not give much guidance as to which test is preferred, so the law here is somewhat unclear. Denham J. explicitly adopted the *Heaney* test and Murray C.J. used a very similar test, so it would appear that this is the preferred test. Fennelly J. expressly stated that no separate proportionality test was required and that it could be accommodated within the existing *Keegan/O'Keeffe* reasonableness test (on which, see Ch.6). The court in *Efe v Minister for Justice* [2011] IEHC 214 found that the effect of *Meadows* was to create a general proportionality test, the factors of which are assessed below.

RATIONAL CONNECTION

Rational connection means that an administrative measure must be rationally connected to the objective. It cannot be arbitrary, unfair or irrational. In *Limerick Corp v Sheridan* (1956) 90 I.L.T.R. 59, Limerick Corporation enacted a byelaw under the Local Government Act 1948 which prohibited the construction of any temporary dwelling 300 yards from the centre of any street. The objective was probably to deal with the problem of unsanitary itinerant settlements. However, in effect, it outlawed all temporary dwellings anywhere, including people camping in their gardens or harvesters camping in the fields where they worked. It was therefore in excess of what was required to achieve that particular objective.

In *R. v Oakes* [1986] 1 S.C.R. 103, the applicant had been found with eight vials of hashish oil and wanted to challenge the Narcotic Control Act 1970, which placed the burden of proof on him to prove he was not a drug dealer. The Canadian Supreme Court found that there is a three-step test which must be passed to justify a limitation on a person's rights. The court articulated the test as follows:

"At a minimum, an objective must relate to societal concerns which are pressing and substantial in a free and democratic society before it can be characterized as sufficiently important. Second, the party invoking s.1 must show the means to be reasonable and demonstrably justified. This involves a form of proportionality test involving three important components. To begin, the measures must be fair and not arbitrary, carefully designed to achieve the objective in question and rationally connected to that objective. In addition, the means should impair the right in question as little as possible. Lastly, there must be a proportionality between the effects of the limiting measure and the objective—the more severe the deleterious effects of a measure, the more important the objective must be."

The court found that the reverse onus of proof did not pass the rational connection test:

"Possession of a small or negligible quantity of narcotics does not support the inference of trafficking ... it would be irrational to infer that a person had an intent to traffic on the basis of his or her possession of a very small quantity of narcotics."

Therefore, s.8 of the Narcotic Control Act was in violation of the Canadian Charter of Rights and Freedoms and was of no force or effect.

LEAST RESTRICTIVE MEANS

This requirement means that an administrative measure should result in as little impairment as possible on the rights of citizens. Unfortunately, there is no Irish case law on the requirement that measures "impair the right as little as possible". In *Shelton v Tucker* 364 US 479; 81 S. Ct. 247; 5 L. Ed. 2d 231 (1960), the US Supreme Court applied the "least restrictive means" test to an Arkansas statute which required teachers to file an affidavit every year which listed all the organisations to which they belonged, and the amount of money they had contributed to each organisation in the previous five years. The plaintiff was one of a group of teachers who refused to do so and, as a result, did not have their teaching contracts renewed. The US Supreme Court found that States had a legitimate interest in investigating the fitness and competence of their teachers, and that the information requested in the affidavit could help in this investigation. The court found, however, that the statute went far beyond this legitimate purpose when it required information that bore no relationship to a teacher's occupational fitness. The statute was struck down because its "unlimited and indiscriminate sweep" went far beyond the State's legitimate interest in the fitness of its teachers.

Re Guardian News and Media Ltd [2010] 2 A.C. 697 concerned a number of anonymous persons against whom the Treasury had made directions under the Terrorism (United Nations Measures) Order 2006 (S.I. No. 2657 of 2006). When these directions were appealed, several media organisations applied for the anonymity orders to be discharged in order to allow them to fully report the proceedings. The media organisations claimed keeping the identity of the parties anonymous was a disproportionate infringement of the media organisations' right to freedom of expression guaranteed by art.10 of the European Convention on Human Rights (ECHR). The application was resisted by those against whom the directions had been made on the ground that the anonymity orders were necessary to protect their article 8 rights to respect for private and family life. It was found that the "least restrictive means" test was satisfied, as there was only a limited restriction on the media's right to freedom of expression. The media were free to report the details of the case and the full issues involved, but anonymity was a convenient device to meet the real concerns of the appellants whilst at the same time preserving an open hearing.

In *R. (F) v Secretary of State for the Home Department* [2011] 1 A.C. 311, the applicants were subject to an indefinite requirement to inform the police of their personal details and foreign travel plans under the Sexual Offences Act 2003. It was held that this was a disproportionate interference with their rights under art.8 of the ECHR to respect for private and family life, because there was no provision for individual review. In *R. (Daly) v Secretary of State* [2001] 2 A.C. 532, a prisoner challenged prison rules under which cells were searched and correspondence was examined in order to secure prison safety. The inmates were required to be absent during those searches in order to prevent intimidation of prison officers and to prevent them from becoming familiar with search techniques. The applicant kept correspondence with his lawyer in his cell and claimed that the rules amounted to an infringement of his right to legal professional privilege, and to respect for the privacy of communications under art.8 of the ECHR. The House of Lords held that the objective of preventing intimidation could be achieved by less intrusive means, although it could be justified in cases where prisoners were disruptive.

THE EFFECT ON RIGHTS IS PROPORTIONATE TO THE OBJECTIVE

Every administrative measure will result in some impact on somebody's rights. As discussed above, this should be the minimum amount of impact necessary; however, even the minimum level of impact on a person's rights may still be quite severe. Therefore, the effect on those rights must be proportionate to the objective of the measure. This was considered in *Daly v Revenue Commissioners* [1995] 3 I.R. 1, where it was held that the test of proportionality could be stated as follows:

> "1. the objective of the impugned provision must be of sufficient importance to warrant over-riding a constitutionally protected right, and must relate to concerns pressing and substantial in a free and democratic society;

2. the means chosen must be rationally connected to the objective and not be arbitrary, unfair or based on irrational considerations; they must impair the right as little as possible; and must be such that their effect on the right was proportional to the objective."

In *Enright v Ireland* [2003] 2 I.R. 321, it was claimed that placing a sex offender on the sex offenders' register was disproportionate. Sex offenders are obliged to provide their address to the Gardaí and to notify them if they are changing address or leaving the State. It was held that the infringement of rights was minimal—the plaintiff did not have restrictions on his movement or was not subject to far-reaching notification provisions like those found in U.S. legislation. The legislation in question—s.7(2) of the Sex Offenders Act 2001—was upheld as being proportionate to the objective of protecting the public from sex offenders who may re-offend.

In *Minister for Justice v Ostrowski* [2012] IEHC 57, Edwards J. refused to order the surrender to Poland, on foot of a European arrest warrant, of a Polish national, holding that it was a disproportionate interference with his rights. The Polish authorities were seeking to prosecute him for the possession of 0.72 grams of marijuana. Edwards J. found:

"I have not been satisfied overall that it would be a proportionate measure to order the surrender of the respondent on foot of the European arrest warrant presently before me. I have concluded rather that in the particular circumstances of the respondent's case it would represent a disproportionate interference with his fundamental rights, and particularly his right to liberty, his right to enjoy physical and mental health, and his right to respect for family life, to surrender him at this time."

This was appealed to the Supreme Court ([2013] IESC 324), where the decision of Edwards J. was reversed. Denham C.J. held that proportionality does not apply to the European arrest warrant system, as proportionality is a matter to be considered by the issuing State rather than by the Irish courts. She stated:

"The matter of member states issuing EAWs for trivial offences is a matter which may be addressed. However, it cannot be addressed by the courts exercising a proportionality test. It is an issue which should be addressed in another forum."

Denham C.J. further stated:

"Even if the principle of proportionality might arise in some circum-stances, even if it could be a factor in a case, there is no basis in the principle of proportionality upon which to refuse to surrender the respondent in this case."

THE PROPORTIONALITY DOCTRINE ONLY APPLIES WHERE A MEASURE INTERFERES WITH A PROTECTED RIGHT

The proportionality principle only tests the legality of measures which interfere with personal rights protected by either the Constitution or the ECHR. In *McCann v Minister for Education* [1997] 1 I.L.R.M. 1, the applicant challenged the Minister for Education's rules which decided which secondary school teachers would be entitled to incremental salaries. To be recognised as an art teacher, a teacher had to have undertaken a course in art at a recognised school of art, followed by a one-year course in teacher training. The applicant had undertaken a three-year course in art at a teacher training college, and not at a school of art. Although she taught continually for 17 years at the same school, she never received an incremental increase. The High Court rejected the argument that the rules infringed the "least restrictive means" component of the proportionality test, as none of the applicant's rights were affected. An incremental salary is not a legally protected right—it is a privilege. The proportionality test cannot be extended to administrative orders, measures, decisions or regulations which do not attack legally protected rights. In *O'Reilly v O'Sullivan and Dún Laoghaire* [1996] IEHC 6, Laffoy J. held:

> "The rationale underlying the principle of proportionality is the protection of constitutional rights by requiring that any restriction on the exercise of those rights permitted by law passes a proportionality test. In this case, there is no evidence whatsoever that the invocation of the 'emergency' procedure infringed a constitutionally protected right of any of the Applicants."

CONCLUSION

The exact position of the proportionality test is uncertain. It was given a resounding endorsement by the Supreme Court in *Meadows*, where it was found that a lack of proportionality was one of the grounds under which a decision could be found to be unreasonable. However, the Supreme Court judges gave differing views on proportionality in that case. It does appear from the case law, in particular, the judgment of McKechnie J. in the Supreme Court in *Ostrowski*, that the *Heaney* test is still the preferred method for assessing proportionality. McKechnie J. found that, in 20 years, the doctrine had not changed in its essential substance. Unfortunately, whilst he made reference to the decision in *Meadows*, he did not comment upon it, as it was not relied upon by the parties in the case.

Legitimate Expectation

9

INTRODUCTION

Legitimate expectation is the doctrine of administrative law which applies the principles of fairness and reasonableness to the situation where an applicant has an interest in a public body complying with an undertaking, or keeping up a long-standing practice. If a legitimate expectation has been breached, a public body can be compelled to follow certain procedural steps, either because it has done so in the past or because it has indicated to the person that such a procedure would be followed in his case. When considering legitimate expectation applications, the courts must strike a balance between upholding the rights of citizens and giving effect to the intentions of the Oireachtas. Like the doctrine of proportionality, this doctrine originated in Germany, where it is a principle of constitutional law, and made its way into Irish law via our European neighbours. It is a purely administrative remedy—it only applies to public bodies and cannot be used between two private parties (*Duggan v An Taoiseach* [1989] I.L.R.M. 713).

ORIGIN

Legitimate expectation entered Irish law in the landmark case of *Webb v Ireland* [1988] I.R. 353 which arose out of the discovery of a hoard of treasure in Derrynaflan, Co. Tipperary. Finlay C.J. found in that case that legitimate expectation is an aspect of promissory estoppel. Promissory estoppel is the equitable concept where, in certain circumstances, a promise or representation may be binding on the promisor or representor. The relationship between legitimate expectation and promissory estoppel was explained by McCracken J. in *Abrahamson v Law Society of Ireland* [1996] 1 I.R. 403:

> "While there is no doubt that the doctrine of legitimate expectation is similar to and probably founded upon the equitable concept of promissory estoppels ... it has in fact been extended well beyond the bounds of that doctrine. Promissory estoppel is largely defensive in its nature, and has been described as 'a shield and not a sword'. Its use is basically to ensure that a person who has made a representation

that they will not exercise some legitimate right is in fact bound by that expectation, and cannot exercise the right. Furthermore, it is usually, although not exclusively, related to matters of private law rather than public law."

Legitimate expectation was described by O'Hanlon J. in *Fakih v Minister for Justice* [1993] 2 I.R. 406 as having some of the characteristics of an "unruly horse" associated with the plea of public policy. By this, he meant that it had quickly developed beyond its original purpose.

PRECONDITIONS FOR LEGITIMATE EXPECTATION

The current leading case on legitimate expectation is *Glencar Exploration v Mayo CC* [2002] 1 I.R. 84. There, Fennelly J. set out the three preconditions which must be met in order to raise a legitimate expectation:

1. The public authority must have made a statement or adopted a position amounting to a promise or representation, express or implied, as to how it would act in respect of an identifiable area of its activity.
2. This representation must be addressed or conveyed either directly or indirectly to an identifiable person or group of persons, affected actually or potentially, in such a way that it formed part of a transaction definitively entered into, or a relationship between that person or group and the public authority, or the person or group had acted on the faith of the representation.
3. It must be such as to create an expectation reasonably entertained by the person or group that the public authority will abide by the representation to the extent that it would be unjust to permit the public authority to resile from it.

THE SOURCES OF LEGITIMATE EXPECTATION

THERE MUST BE AN UNDERTAKING

The conduct of the administrative body must have been sufficiently clear to have generated an undertaking. In *Wiley v Revenue Commissioners* [1989] I.R. 350, it was found that the erroneous repayment of excise duty and VAT on a car to a disabled driver on two occasions may have given him a reasonable belief that it would be repaid again, but it fell far short of constituting an undertaking which could form the basis of a legitimate expectation.

In *Cosgrave v DPP* [2012] IESC 24, the applicant claimed that his continued prosecution for corruption charges was an abuse of process and a breach of his legitimate expectations. The High Court was of the view that the failure to disclose a witness statement did not amount to the adoption of a position, a promise or a representation. The judge remarked: "It seems to me that to suggest that this non-disclosure amounted to a representation would be to stretch the meaning of *Glencar* far beyond its true meaning." On appeal to the Supreme Court, this was affirmed in full.

Express Undertakings

In the English case of *R. (Greenpeace) v Secretary of State for Trade* [2007] EWHC 311 (Admin), an undertaking was given by the English Government in a white paper on energy policy in 2003. It undertook not to pursue nuclear power as a priority and that nuclear power would only be pursued following "the fullest public consultation and the publication of a white paper setting out the Government's proposals". In 2006, the Secretary of State published a report in which it was announced that the Government had changed its policy and now favoured building new nuclear power stations. The public were not informed in advance that the Government was considering changing its policy. Greenpeace challenged the change of policy on the basis that the promised consultation process had not been followed and that there was a legitimate expectation that it would be. The court found that there was a legitimate expectation and that this expectation had been breached, rendering the new policy unlawful. Similarly, in *Glenkerrin Homes v Dún Laoghaire–Rathdown CC* [2011] 1 I.R. 417, the applicant was held to have had a legitimate expectation that the relevant policy in that case would not change without reasonable notice having been given.

In *John M.P. Greaney Ltd v Dublin Corp* [1994] 3 I.R. 384, the applicant was a limited company specialising in fire safety, design and management. It had made an application to the respondents for a fire safety certificate for work done in upgrading the fire safety measures in a convent in Dublin. It was proposed to convert part of this convent into a marketing and design college. The company was told that it would be contacted in the event of any problem arising with the application. Morris J. held that the applicant was not entitled to claim a legitimate expectation unless it could be proved that an unqualified assurance was given which formed an integral part of the transaction, or that the conduct of notifying applicants of problems with the application was so well-established, regular and so well-founded that the courts should give effect to it.

Long-standing Practice

In *Sherlock v Governor of Mountjoy Prison* [1991] 1 I.R. 451, the applicant was a convicted murderer who had been allowed temporary release from prison on 15 occasions over a period of 12 years. He had always complied with the terms of his release but was told after his last release that he would no longer be granted temporary release. It was held that the applicant had a legitimate expectation that temporary release would be continued and that he had to be given the opportunity to make representations against the reversal of the long-standing practice in order for the revocation of his temporary release to be lawful. The High Court did not order the grant of further temporary release but it did order the Minister to give the applicant the reasons why the temporary release was not being renewed and to afford him an opportunity of dealing with these reasons.

An example where a claim for legitimate expectation based on a long-standing practice was unsuccessful is *Egan v Minister for Defence*, unreported, High Court, Barr J., November 24, 1988. The applicant was an officer of the air corps who was seeking permission to take early retirement in order to join a commercial airline following 24 years' service. There had been a long-standing practice that officers of five years' standing would be given permission to retire early upon an application to the Minister for Defence. Permission to retire was refused to the applicant in this case. The court held that not only was there no such practice on the Minister's part which might give rise to a legitimate expectation, but that the Minister's refusal was reasonable as there had been numerous applications by air corps pilots for early retirement and there would be difficulty in maintaining a viable air corps if they were all granted.

In *Glenkerrin Homes Ltd v Dún Laoghaire–Rathdown CC* [2011] 1 I.R. 417, Clarke J. found that:

> "An implied representation can derive from the universal following of a particular practice for a prolonged period of time. It is, of course, important to note that the executive enjoys a constitutional entitlement to change policy. Furthermore, bodies exercising a statutory role (such as the defendant in this case) also enjoy an entitlement to alter the policy within which they exercise their statutory functions, subject only to the overall requirement that whatever policies are adopted must be consistent with their statutory role as defined. It is clear, therefore, that a legitimate expectation cannot arise to the effect that a policy will not be changed ... I should, therefore, emphasise that the existence of a longstanding practice does not give rise to any legitimate expectation that that practice will not change."

CIRCULARS

Circulars are documents issued by Government Departments and they can be the source of a legitimate expectation. In *Power v Minister for Social and Family Affairs* [2007] 1 I.R. 543, the applicants were social welfare recipients who were induced to enrol in full-time higher education by a back-to-work scheme administered by the respondent's Department. The scheme was promoted by an information booklet. The information booklet stated that payments under the scheme continued during all academic holiday periods. In 2003, the Department withdrew the payment of the allowance during the summer holidays. The High Court held that the information booklet conveyed a representation to an identifiable group of people and had the effect of making the Department accountable under the doctrine of legitimate expectation.

In *Keogh v Criminal Assets Bureau* [2004] 2 I.R. 159, the second-named respondents—the Revenue Commissioners—gave a specific undertaking in the taxpayers' charter of rights that fair procedures required the furnishing of full, timely and accurate information on the provisions of revenue law to all taxpayers with whom they had dealings, informing them of their entitlements and obligations. In 1996, the Gardaí had seized money from the applicant's house on which traces of cannabis and cocaine were found. The applicant agreed to pay this money over to the first-named respondent, and the Revenue Commissioners contacted him about his tax affairs. He was not informed of his rights and obligations under tax law, in particular, his right of appeal. It was claimed that the charter of rights gave him a legitimate expectation that he should be informed of his rights; however, he was unaware of the existence of the charter. Keane C.J. noted:

> "It is undoubtedly the case that documents such as the charter of rights under consideration in the present case, whether so described or called a 'mission statement' or given some other title, frequently contain what are no more than praiseworthy statements of an aspirational nature, designed to encourage the members of the organisation concerned to meet acceptable standards of behaviour in their dealings with the public and to give the latter some form of assurance that complaints as to discourtesy or other shortcomings on the part of the former will be seriously entertained. Some at least of the undertakings in the taxpayers' charter of rights would fall into that category. Statements of that nature would not normally give rise to causes of action based on the legitimate expectation doctrine."

The Supreme Court allowed his appeal but, unfortunately, did not consider it necessary to consider whether or not the failure to inform the applicant of his rights amounted to a breach of a legitimate expectation or simply a breach of fair procedure.

INTERNATIONAL TREATIES

The circumstances in which an international treaty can give rise to a legitimate expectation appear to be limited. In particular, such an expectation cannot operate so as to conflict with an Irish statute or with the Constitution. In *Kavanagh v Mountjoy Prison* [2002] 3 I.R. 97, it was claimed that the applicant had a legitimate expectation that the International Covenant on Civil and Political Rights would be complied with, and that being tried in the Special Criminal court violated this. The High Court held that there could be no legitimate expectation of a substantive right which would conflict with the statute law of the State or the Constitution, or with the well-established principles of the common law. The Supreme Court dismissed the appeal against the High Court's decision and added that the doctrine of legitimate expectation does not guarantee anything more than procedural fairness. Depending on the circumstances, it may be conceivable that the application of the legitimate expectation doctrine would have the effect of conferring rights, but that would be an indirect consequence.

In *Grierosu v DPP* [2008] 3 I.R. 732, the applicant had been prosecuted for presenting a fake passport when she arrived in Ireland, which she alleged was contrary to the UN Refugee Convention. That Convention provides that a Contracting State will not impose penalties on refugees on account of their illegal entry if they come directly from a territory where their life or freedom was threatened, and present themselves without delay to the authorities showing good cause for their illegal entry. The applicant contended that she had a legitimate expectation that the DPP would consider her request to have the proceedings withdrawn. It was found that the expectation conflicted not only with statute, but also with Art.30.3 of the Constitution, as it would fetter the DPP's discretion.

OTHER ELEMENTS OF LEGITIMATE EXPECTATION

THE EXPECTATION MUST BE LEGITIMATE

It is not enough to show that an expectation exists: it must also be legitimate—that is, an expectation which is reasonably entertained. Relief will be refused where the expectation is unreasonable. In *R. (Iqbal) v Secretary of State for the Home Department* [2006] EWHC 3048 (Admin), the applicant had applied for asylum and was refused. In 2005, he received a letter, generated as a result of a computer error, which informed him that he had been granted asylum. It said:

"Following confirmation that your application for asylum has been determined and the confirmation that you have been granted leave to remain in the United Kingdom, I am writing to advise you that you no longer qualify for support under section 95 of the Immigration and Asylum Act 1999.

The support that you have been provided with is to be discontinued. Support is provided for a period of 28 days following the notification of the resolution of your asylum claim, which is deemed to be received 2 days following the determination of your asylum application. Our records show that your claim for asylum was determined on the 26th October 2001, therefore the period of support ended on 24th November 2001."

He then claimed the letter had created a legitimate expectation that he would be granted leave to remain in the United Kingdom. The High Court rejected the claim as the letter was inconsistent with all of the other indications. Further, the applicant had not engaged in correspondence with the respondent. Under the circumstances, the expectation was not legitimate. This case can be contrasted with the Irish decision in *VI v Commissioner of An Garda Síochána* [2007] 4 I.R. 47, where a similar letter from the Department of Justice was found to create a legitimate expectation.

In *Fairleigh v Temple Bar Renewal Ltd* [1990] 2 I.R. 508, it was held that, despite the relationship between the applicant and respondent, there was nothing which could give rise to a legitimate expectation that an approval for a licensed premises in Temple Bar would be forthcoming. The provisions of the Temple Bar Area Renewal and Development Act 1991 obliged the respondent to refuse approval where it was of the opinion that granting approval would be detrimental to a suitable mix of users and activity in the area. The court found, therefore, that it was not reasonable for the applicant to have expected that an approval would be forthcoming.

THE PERSON MAKING THE REPRESENTATION MUST HAVE AUTHORITY

The person who makes the representation which is relied upon must have the authority to make it. If a representation is made by someone who does not have the requisite authority, it will not be binding on the public body. In *South Bucks District Council v Flanagan* [2002] 1 W.L.R. 2601, Keene L.J. held that:

"Legitimate expectation involves notions of fairness and unless the person making the representation has actual or ostensible authority to speak on behalf of the public body, there is no reason why the recipient of the representation should be allowed to hold the public body to the terms of the representation. He might subjectively have acquired the expectation, but it would not be a legitimate one, that is to say it would not be one to which he was entitled."

In *Kenny v Kelly* [1988] 1 I.R. 457, the applicant was offered and accepted a place to study Arts in University College Dublin. Her father was told by the senior administrative officer in the admissions office that she could defer the place for a year. When she returned a year later, she was told the official had gotten her instructions wrong and exceeded her authority, and that the place was not available for her. Despite the fact that the admissions office had no power to grant a deferral, Barron J. found there was a legitimate expectation.

RELIANCE AND CHANGE OF POSITION

Although a person who seeks to reply upon an expectation must be aware of it, he need not have relied on it to his detriment, as is the case in promissory estoppel. In *Galvin v Chief Appeals Officer* [1997] 3 I.R. 240, the court noted that the English case law indicates that an applicant for judicial review may rely on an expectation legitimately held by him, even though he did not act to his detriment. However, this did not arise in that case as the law did not permit the payment of the benefit claimed by the applicant. The Supreme Court in *Daly v Minister for the Marine* [2001] 3 I.R. 513 addressed the issue of whether an expectation, on which there was no reliance, could generate a legitimate expectation. The court said that there was no rule against enforcement in such cases. Even where there was no reliance, an undertaking might be binding, but only where not to recognise the undertaking would be "unfair, discriminatory or unjust".

LEGITIMATE EXPECTATION DOES NOT APPLY TO LEGISLATION

As seen above when discussing international treaties, a legitimate expectation cannot overrule a statute. In *Pesca Valentia Ltd v Minister for Fisheries* [1990] 2 I.R. 305, it was argued that there was a legitimate expectation that no legislative changes would be made affecting the applicant's rights to fish. This was rejected by Keane J., who said:

"While the plaintiffs were undoubtedly encouraged in their project by semi state bodies ... No such 'estoppel' could conceivably operate so as to prevent the Oireachtas from legislating or the executive from implementing the legislation as enacted."

In *Cork Opera House Plc v Revenue Commissioners* [2007] IEHC 388, the applicant claimed that the Revenue Commissioners had the power to grant it a licence to sell alcohol under the Excise Act 1835, and that, therefore, it did not need to apply for a licence in the District Court, as is the norm. It transpired that only theatres established by Royal Patent could use this procedure. The applicant then claimed that, even so, it still had a legitimate expectation that the Revenue Commissioners would continue to act as they had done for many years, incorrectly granting licences under the Excise Act 1835. Hedigan J. held that:

> "Legitimate expectation cannot prevail against a statute. It cannot operate to confer upon a statutory authority a power which that authority does not have under the terms of the relevant statute."

LEGITIMATE EXPECTATION AND THE ULTRA VIRES DOCTRINE

The doctrine of legitimate expectation is potentially in conflict with another doctrine of public law—the ultra vires doctrine (on which, see Ch.3). The ultra vires doctrine prevents authorities from acting beyond their powers. An expectation, even a legitimate one, cannot force an authority to act in a way in which it has no power to act. In *Re Green Dale Building Co* [1977] I.R. 256, the Supreme Court held that estoppel did not apply because it would destroy the doctrine of ultra vires if someone exercising statutory power could extend the power by creating an estoppel. This case pre-dated the introduction of legitimate expectation, but was applied to the doctrine of legitimate expectation in *Galvin v Chief Appeals Officer* [1997] 3 I.R. 240.

SUBSTANTIVE BENEFIT VERSUS PROCEDURAL BENEFIT

Legitimate expectations may be of two kinds:

(a) A procedural expectation: the expectation that a procedure will be followed in the applicant's case.
(b) A substantive expectation: an expectation that a discretionary power will be exercised in the applicant's favour.

The extent to which the expectation will be enforced depends on the type of expectation. Traditionally, the second category is less likely to be enforced as it is conditional and the courts do not wish to fetter an administrator's statutorily-conferred discretion. A public authority is entitled to reverse an expectation if it feels that it is in the public interest, and the reversal can only be stopped if it is unreasonable. In *Abrahamson v Law Society of Ireland* [1996] 1 I.R. 403, the court held:

> "Where the legitimate expectation is that a benefit will be secured, the courts will endeavour to obtain that benefit or to compensate the applicant, whether by way of order of mandamus or by an award of damages, provided that to do so was lawful.
>
> Where a Minister or a public body is given by statute or statutory instrument a discretion or a power to make regulations for the good of the public or a very specific section of the public, the court will not interfere with the exercise of such discretion or power, as to do so would be tantamount to the court usurping that discretion or power to itself, and would be an undue interference by the court in the affairs of the persons or bodies to whom or to which such discretion or power was given by the legislature."

In *Tara Prospecting v Minister for Energy* [1993] I.L.R.M. 771, Costello J. said:

> "In cases involving the exercise of a discretionary statutory power, the only legitimate expectation relating to the conferring of a benefit that can be inferred from words or conduct is a conditional one, namely, that a benefit will be conferred provided that at the time the minister considers that it is a proper exercise of the statutory power, in light of the current policy, to grant it. Such a conditional expectation cannot give rise to an enforceable right to the benefit should it later be refused by the minister in the public interest."

This approach was criticised in *Glencar*, where Keane C.J. said of the above dicta:

> "It has been said that this is an unduly restrictive approach and that there is no reason, in logic or principle, why the doctrine cannot be successfully invoked so as to declare a person entitled, in an appropriate case, not simply to fair procedures, but to the benefit which he was seeking in the particular case."

In the High Court decision in *Lett & Co Ltd v Wexford Borough Corp* [2007] IEHC 195, the court declared mussel fishermen to be entitled to the substantive benefit of compensation, as the source of the benefit claimed was not statutory in origin, and therefore not subject to the usual restriction. The plaintiff did not receive damages for breach of expectation but instead received the compensation to which it had a legitimate expectation. This was relied upon in *Atlantic Marine Supplies & Rogers v Minister for Transport* [2010] IEHC 104. *Lett* was appealed to the Supreme Court ([2012] IESC 14) but, unfortunately, the issue of substantive expectations was not addressed by the Supreme Court.

DAMAGES IN LEGITIMATE EXPECTATION

Traditionally, the result of a legitimate expectation case was that the applicant would be given a procedural or substantive benefit to which he felt he was entitled. It is now clear that damages may be awarded in legitimate expectation cases. In *Lett & Co v Wexford Borough Council* [2012] IESC 14, O'Donnell J. held that "there is sufficient authority and principle to justify a court, once it has determined that there has been a breach of a legitimate expectation, to give such remedy as the equity of the case may demand". If it is not possible to secure the benefit to which the applicant had an expectation, damages will be awarded instead in order to compensate the applicant. In *Abrahamson v Law Society of Ireland* [1996] 1 I.R. 403, McCracken J. found that:

> "Where the legitimate expectation is that a benefit will be secured, the courts will endeavour to obtain that benefit or to compensate the applicant, whether by way of order of *mandamus* or by an award of damages provided that to do so was lawful."

The most obvious case where damages will be awarded is where the expectation was that money would be paid. In *Duff v Minister for Agriculture (No. 2)* [1997] 2 I.R. 22, damages were awarded to farmers who had substantially increased their milk production on foot of a 1972 EEC Directive, only to have their production limited by a super levy on surplus milk introduced by an EC Regulation in 1984.

Finally, damages will also be awarded where there has been a breach of a legitimate expectation, but where to enforce the expectation would be futile. In *Hennessy v St Gerard's School Trust* [2003] IEHC 49, a teacher claimed she had a legitimate expectation to a hearing before the school's board of governors before they made a decision on her application for a teaching post. The court found that even if she had received a hearing, the decision of the board to refuse her the position was unlikely to have been any different. However, she was awarded €15,000 in damages for breach of contract and breach of legitimate expectation. Damages for a breach of a legitimate expectation were expressly upheld by the Supreme Court in *McGrath v Minister for Defence* [2010] 1 I.R. 560, where Geoghegan J. held that the respondent was "entitled to succeed in his claim for damages for breach of legitimate expectation".

Conclusion

Legitimate expectation is now firmly established in Irish law and the position has been clarified by *Glencar.* It has developed from an offshoot of equity into a purely administrative doctrine of its own.

Introduction to Judicial Review

INTRODUCTION

"In the course of the last two decades, throughout the common law world, there has been an explosion in litigation by way of judicial review." So began the judgment of Denham J. (as she then was) in *Dekra Éireann Teo. v Minister for the Environment* [2003] 2 I.R. 270. A judicial review is one of the most common forms of cases taken in Ireland, with around one-third of cases brought in the High Court being judicial reviews. As a result, judicial review is something every legal practitioner must become familiar with, particularly as judicial review is an effective manner of striking down acts or decisions which were incorrectly made.

WHAT IS JUDICIAL REVIEW?

Judicial review is the way by which the judiciary review the acts of administrators, such as lower courts. If those actions are valid, they will be upheld, and if they are invalid, the reviewing court will quash them. Judicial review only applies to matters of public law. In *Meadows v Minister for Justice, Equality and Law Reform* [2010] 2 I.R. 701, Murray C.J. explained that:

> "Judicial review is concerned with the Courts exercising their constitutional duty to ensure that powers, governmental and administrative, are exercised within the law and the Constitution and, inter alia, in a manner consistent with the rights of individuals affected by them. In exercising its jurisdiction to judicially review acts or decisions of the other branches of the Government the Courts must, of course, respect the powers and functions conferred on the executive and the parliament by the Constitution and by law. As I stated in *T.D. & Ors v Minister for Education and Others* [2000] 3 IR 62 'judicial review permits the Courts to place limits on the exercise of executive or legislative power not to exercise it themselves'."

Judicial review does not look at the merits of any decision which is taken, but instead looks at the way in which a decision was reached or an act was done, and it will strike it down if the manner in which it was done breaches any of the rules of administrative law. This form of action can only be taken in the High Court, although it can be appealed to the Supreme Court. Judicial review is a discretionary remedy; this means, according to O'Higgins C.J. in *State (Abenglen Properties Ltd) v Dublin Corp* [1984] I.R. 381, that: "… a person whose legal rights have been infringed may be awarded certiorari … but the court retains a discretion to refuse his application if his conduct has been such as to disentitle him to the relief". Acts such as delay may result in the discretion to refuse an application being exercised. In practice, judicial review is often referred to by the shorthand "JR".

WHAT WILL THIS SECTION OF THE BOOK COVER?

This section of the book (Chs 11–18) will look into the mechanics of judicial review. A judicial review should be available if any of the principles of administrative law dealt with in the preceding chapters of this book are breached. This section will analyse: first, who and what can be subject to judicial review; secondly, the procedure behind getting a decision judicially reviewed; thirdly, who can bring a judicial review, how long they have to bring a judicial review and the discretionary bars which may prevent them from doing so; and, finally, the matters of costs and remedies will be dealt with.

Who and What can be Subject to Judicial Review?

INTRODUCTION

When examining who and what can be subject to judicial review, we have to look at the limits of judicial review. Not every organisation is going to be subject to judicial review. Further, even if an organisation is generally subject to judicial review, not all of its decisions or acts can be the subject of judicial review, as public law does not apply to everything a public body does. For example, were a District Court judge to run you over in his car, or if An Bord Pleanála breached a contract with you, private law remedies found in the laws of tort and contract would be more appropriate. As a general rule, any person or body exercising a public function may be subject to judicial review. In Ireland, the law governing who and what is subject to judicial review is more liberal and expansive than in other jurisdictions. This is due to the decision in *Geoghegan v Institute of Chartered Accountants* [1995] 3 I.R. 86.

THE TEST TO SEE IF JUDICIAL REVIEW IS AVAILABLE AS A REMEDY

Judicial review originated as a remedy against lower courts, as it is part of the function of the superior courts to control the judicial processes of the lower courts (*State (Abenglen Properties Ltd) v Dublin Corp* [1984] I.R. 381). The lower courts include the District Court and the Circuit Court. If one of these courts acts in excess of its jurisdiction, it can be judicially reviewed in the superior courts (*Ruttlege v District Judge Clyne* [2006] IEHC 146). Judicial review was extended to other bodies long ago. In *R. v Electricity Commissioner* [1924] 1 K.B. 171, Lord Atkin recognised that judicial review was not just confined to courts of justice, but could apply to any body with authority under statute. The test to see whether a body's decision can be judicially reviewed has developed over time, allowing more bodies to be reviewed than was originally the case.

Traditional Test—Source of the Power

Traditionally, when deciding if judicial review was available as a remedy, the courts examined the relationship between the applicant and the decision-maker to determine the source of the decision-maker's power. If the applicant had voluntarily submitted to the authority of the decision maker (for example, by entering into a contract with it), then the source of the decision-maker's power was a private law matter, and public law remedies such as judicial review were not available.

In *State (Colquhoun) v D'Arcy* [1936] I.R. 641, it was found that a decision by the Court of the General Synod of the Church of Ireland to discipline a minister was not subject to judicial review, as that court derived its authority solely from the consent or agreement of the church members rather than from a statute. The High Court found that judicial review would only issue to a court, tribunal or body of persons that:

(a) has a duty to act judicially;
(b) has authority to impose liabilities or to determine questions which affect the rights of individuals, and;
(c) derives authority from statute or common law.

In *Murphy v Turf Club* [1989] I.R. 172, the applicant was a racehorse trainer seeking to review a decision by the horse racing governing body to revoke his training licence. This decision effectively terminated his ability to earn a livelihood. The court found that the relationship between the applicant and the respondent derived solely from contract and that the respondent's duty to regulate the sport of horse racing in Ireland, although it had a public dimension, was not a public duty. Therefore, the decision could not be judicially reviewed as the applicant had voluntarily submitted to the respondent's jurisdiction.

Current Approach—Public Element Test

The courts' approach has changed over time. The source of the power is still important but it no longer completely determines the issue. The courts now also look to the nature of the power and, in particular, whether there is a public element to the decision. A decision can have a public element even if only one individual is affected by it. This approach was first used by the Supreme Court in *Beirne v Commissioner of An Garda Síochána* [1993] I.L.R.M. 1. In that case, the applicant was a trainee Garda whose assignment was terminated because of alleged misconduct. He claimed the investigation into the alleged misconduct breached his right to fair procedures as he had not been given a chance to contradict allegations made or to cross-examine the people who had made statements against him. The Garda Commissioner argued that the right to terminate the applicant's assignment came from contract and that, therefore, his decision could not be subject to judicial review as it was a private matter. Finlay C.J. held:

> "The principle which, in general, excludes from the ambit of judicial review decisions made in the realm of private law by persons or tribunals whose authority derives from contract is, I am quite satisfied, confined to cases or instances where the duty being performed by the decision-making authority is manifestly a private duty and where his right to make it derives solely from contract or solely from consent or the agreement of the parties affected.
>
> Where the duty being carried out by a decision-making authority, as occurs in this case, is of a nature which might ordinarily be seen as coming within the public domain, that decision can only be excluded from the reach of the jurisdiction in judicial review if it can be shown that it solely and exclusively derived from an individual contract made in private law."

Even though the Commissioner's power to discipline and dismiss the applicant came from contract, it was clear that the power also came from the office that the Commissioner held, and the statutory powers attached to it. Even though there was a strong contractual element to the relationship, judicial review was available due to this public element.

Beirne was applied in *Browne v Dundalk UDC* [1993] 2 I.R. 512. In that case, Sinn Féin party members had booked a hall from Dundalk Urban District Council for Sinn Féin's annual conference. When the councillors learned of this, they passed a resolution to cancel the contract. Barr J. held that whilst, prima facie, this case appeared to be simply a matter of contract, it was clear that the decision of the councillors was politically motivated, which brought the decision clearly into the public domain. The termination of the contract could be the subject of judicial review, and it was quashed.

The "public element" test was elaborated on in *Eogan v UCD* [1996] I.R. 390. In that case, a number of factors were identified when deciding if a decision could be subject to judicial review:

(a) whether the decision challenged has been made pursuant to a statute;

(b) whether the decision-maker, by its decision, is performing a duty relating to a matter of particular and immediate public concern, and therefore falling within the public domain;

(c) where the decision affects a contract of employment, whether that employment has any statutory protection so as to afford the employee any "public rights" upon which he may rely; and

(d) whether the decision is being made by a decision-maker whose powers, though not directly based on statute, depend on approval by the legislature or the Government for their continued exercise.

One case worth noting is *Rajah v Royal College of Surgeons of Ireland* [1994] 1 I.R. 384. In that case, the applicant sought to judicially review the decision of the academic appeals board of the respondent not to allow her to re-sit exams that she had twice failed. No reasons were given for the decision. Even though the respondent had been established by law—a Royal Charter— the relationship between the parties was found to be purely contractual; as there was no public element, judicial review was therefore not available as a remedy. Similarly, in *Quinn v King's Inns* [2004] 4 I.R. 344, it was held that the relationship between the King's Inns and its students was purely contractual and could not be the subject of judicial review.

THE "*GEOGHEGAN* PRINCIPLES"

The guiding light now as to whether or not a decision can be subject to judicial review comes from the principles established by the Supreme Court in *Geoghegan v Institute of Chartered Accountants* [1995] 3 I.R. 86. This judgment identifies factors which help show whether or not a decision has a public element. The applicant had sought to restrain professional misconduct disciplinary proceedings by the Institute of Chartered Accountants. In the course of her judgment, Denham J. (as she then was) listed the following factors which she took into account:

"In view of the public nature of the source of the Institute, the functions of the Institute, and the nature of the contract between the Appellant and the Institute, the subject of Judicial Review becomes part of the question of constitutional justice of the relationship. There are a number of important factors:—

1. The case relates to a major profession, important in the community, with a special connection to the judicial organ of Government in the courts in areas such as receivership, liquidation, examinership, as well as having special auditing responsibilities.

2. The original source of the powers of the Institute is the Charter: through that and legislation and the procedure to alter and amend

the bye-laws, the Institute had a nexus with two branches of the Government of the State.

3. The functions of the Institute and its members come within the public domain of the State.

4. The method by which the contractual relationship between the Institute and the applicant was created is an important factor as it was necessary for the individual to agree in a 'form' contract to the disciplinary process to gain entrance to membership of the Institute.

5. The consequences of the domestic tribunal's decision may be very serious for a member.

6. The proceedings before the Disciplinary Committee must be fair and in accordance with the principles of natural justice, it must act judicially."

Although Denham J.'s judgment in *Geoghegan* was in the minority, these principles were relied upon in the subsequent High Court cases of *Rafferty v Bus Éireann* [1997] 2 I.R. 424 and *Bane v Garda Representative Association* [1997] 2 I.R. 449. In *Rafferty*, the applicants were seeking to review changes to their terms of employment following a reorganisation of Córas Iompair Éireann by statute. Kelly J. found that whilst the *Geoghegan* case was dealing with matters entirely different to what he was dealing with, a number of the factors identified by Denham J. were relevant. He held:

"1. This case relates to a major method of public transport and to persons employed in that operation. Public transport is important to the community. Disputes concerning persons employed therein which might give rise to industrial action have consequences of hardship, particularly for members of the community who are entirely dependent upon it.

2. The original provider of the service now being given by Irish Bus, was the statutory corporation, CIE. Irish Bus itself owes its existence to the [Transport (Re-organisation of Córas Iompair Éireann) Act 1986]. Furthermore, it is the Act which places restrictions upon it concerning its employees through Section 14.

3. The functions of Irish Bus and its employees come within the public domain of the State. Although a company formed by registration, I cannot ignore its statutory genesis.

4. The method, by which the contractual relationship between Irish Bus and its employees is regulated, is subject to the statutory intervention which is contained in Section 14 of the Act.

5. The consequences of an unlawful interference with the contractual rights of Irish Bus's employees may be very serious for them."

These five considerations match the matters identified by Denham J. in *Geoghegan*. In Kelly J.'s view, they supported the applicant's entitlement to use judicial review rather than plenary proceedings.

The so-called *Geoghegan* principles were affirmed by the Supreme Court in *O'Donnell v Tipperary (South Riding) CC* [2005] 2 I.R. 483. In that case, the applicant had been dismissed from his position in a fire station. The High Court had found that judicial review was not an appropriate remedy as the power to dismiss was founded in contract. Although the case was dismissed for other reasons, the Supreme Court did find that judicial review was an appropriate remedy. In particular, Denham J. noted that where the respondent was a public authority, the burden of proof rested on it to show that the power to dismiss was solely governed by contract.

NON-STATUTORY BODIES THAT CARRY OUT FUNCTIONS ON BEHALF OF THE STATE

There are two highly influential English decisions which should be noted here. They suggest that if an administrative body carries out functions on behalf of the State, it should be subject to judicial review, even if it was not established by statute.

R. v Criminal Injuries Compensation Board, Ex p. Lain [1967] 2 Q.B. 864— The applicant was seeking compensation for the fatal injury suffered by her husband, a policeman, when he was shot by a suspect. The Criminal Injuries Compensation Board was established by a royal prerogative, as opposed to a statute. Lord Parker C.J. held that the Criminal Injuries Compensation Board is a public body under a duty to act judicially, and is therefore amenable to judicial review:

> "The position as I see it is that the exact limits of the ancient remedy by way of certiorari have never been, and ought not to be, specifically defined. They have varied from time to time, being extended to meet changing conditions ... We have, as it seems to me, reached the position when the ambit of certiorari can be said to cover every case in which a body of persons, of a public as opposed to a purely private or domestic character, has to determine matters affecting subjects provided always that it has a duty to act judicially."

R. v Panel on Takeovers and Mergers, Ex p. Datafin [1987] Q.B. 815—This is one of the leading cases on who can be judicially reviewed. The Court of Appeal held that it may be possible to judicially review a decision-maker who does not have statutory or common law authority. This is possible if the duty imposed on the body, whether expressly or by implication, was a public duty and the body was exercising public law functions. The court no longer had to look at the source of the powers but could look at the nature of the powers. In this case, the respondent Panel— forming part of the British Government's scheme to regulate the City of London's financial markets—regulated take-overs and enforced a code of conduct on them. Those affected had no choice but to submit to the Panel's jurisdiction. As a result, the Panel had the duty to act judicially and its decisions could be judicially reviewed. This case was referred to with approval in Ireland in *Murphy v Turf Club* [1989] I.R. 172, but was found not to apply on the facts. It was also referred to with approval in *Beirne v Commissioner of An Garda Síochána* [1993] I.L.R.M. 1, and was implicitly adopted in *Becker v Duggan* [2005] IEHC 376.

Decisions which may be Judicially Reviewed

Judicial review has been granted in respect of a wide variety of public decisions. These include:

– a failure to keep a court house in proper repair (*State (King) v Minister for Defence* [1984] I.R. 169);
– a disciplinary award made by a prison governor (*Re McKiernan* [1985] N.I. 385);
– the verdict of an inquest (*State (McKeown) v Scully* [1986] I.R. 524);
– the designation of land as an area of scientific interest (*McPharthalain v Commissioners for Public Works* [1994] 3 I.R. 353);
– a refusal to grant a marriage certificate (*Lambert v An tÁrd Chláraitheoir* [1995] 2 I.R. 372);
– a decision to allow a private prosecution (*R. (on the application of Chief Constable of Northumbria) v Newcastle upon Tyne Magistrates' Court* [2010] EWHC 935 (Admin));
– the dismissal of an airman (*Rawson v Minister for Defence* [2012] IESC 26); and
– a decision to free a man from imprisonment for debt, and to suspend all civil actions against him for a limited period (*Lyman v Mower* 2 Vt. 517 (1830)).

The number of situations where judicial review has been permitted is so vast that it is impossible to list them all. Instead, it is easier to examine decisions where judicial review will *not* be permitted.

DECISIONS NOT SUBJECT TO JUDICIAL REVIEW

SUPERIOR COURTS

Judicial review is not a remedy against the decisions of the superior courts. The superior courts are the High Court, the Court of Criminal Appeal and the Supreme Court. The Special Criminal Court is considered a lower court for the purpose of judicial review (*DPP v Special Criminal Court* [1999] 1 I.R. 60). However, judicial review is available against decisions made by officers attached to the High Court such as the Master of the High Court (*Elwyn (Cottons) Ltd v Master of the High Court* [1989] I.R. 14) and the Taxing Master (*Gannon v Flynn* [2001] 3 I.R. 581). Lower courts—the District Court and Circuit Court—can be judicially reviewed. In *State (Freeman) v Connellan* [1986] 1 I.R. 433, it was held that it is undesirable, where judges are being judicially reviewed, for the judges to rely on affidavits made by themselves, as this exposes them to the risk of being cross-examined. It would be more judicious if the affidavit were made by the court clerk or registrar. However, if one of the superior courts breaches one of the principals of administrative law, it can be set aside. In *Kenny v Trinity College* [2008] 1 I.L.R.M. 241, it was found that there was objective bias where a member of the Supreme Court was the brother of a member of a firm of architects whose development was being challenged. The applicant's appeal had originally been disallowed by the Supreme Court, but was re-instated when bias was found.

PRIVATE DECISIONS

As discussed above, unless there is some public element to a private decision, then public law remedies such as judicial review will not be available. Private law deals with the relationships between private individuals whereas public law deals with the relationships between private individuals and emanations of the State. These agencies can wield a vast amount of power over the common citizen and it is the function of the courts to ensure these powers are used correctly, and to protect citizens from their abuse. This power relationship does not apply to private cases, even if one party is in a dominant position over the other.

Decisions of the DPP

The Office of the Director of Public Prosecutions (DPP) was established by s.2 of the Prosecution of Offences Act 1974. Decisions of the DPP to prosecute or not to prosecute can be reviewed, according to the decision in *State (McCormack) v Curran* [1987] I.L.R.M. 225. The DPP's decision can only be reviewed on limited grounds: where the DPP has been influenced by some improper motive or policy; where the DPP has abdicated her functions; or where the DPP has acted mala fides, i.e. in bad faith. These grounds are particularly hard to prove, as, according to the decision in *H v DPP* [1994] 2 I.R. 589, the DPP is not under a duty to provide the reasons why she came to a decision. The only instance where the DPP may be required to make discovery—that is, to give a list of the documents relating to the case in her possession or power of procurement—is where there is evidence of impropriety or a lack of fair procedures in making her decision (*Cunningham v President of the Circuit Court* [2006] 3 I.R. 541). Otherwise, discovery cannot be granted against the DPP (*Dunphy v DPP* [2005] 3 I.R. 385). This, however, may change when the European Directive on Victims Rights (Directive 2012/29, [2012] OJ L315/57) is implemented in Ireland, which will require the DPP to provide reasons for every decision (for further details, see M. Holmes, "The Impact of the Proposed Victims Rights Directive on the Criminal Justice System" (2012) 17(4) B.R. 80).

Government Decisions

It would be a breach of the separation of powers if the judiciary were able to overrule every decision made by the Government. Certain matters—for example, foreign policy—are for the Government to decide, not the judiciary. In *TD v Minister for Education* [2001] 4 I.R. 259, the Supreme Court declined to find that it had any power to compel the Government to implement a particular policy, as this is a matter for the executive and to do so would breach the separation of powers. In *McKenna v An Taoiseach (No. 1)* [1995] 2 I.R. 1, Costello J. declined to interfere with, and quash, a decision by the Government to spend public money supporting a "yes" vote in the Maastricht treaty referendum in 1992. He stated:

> "Not every grievance can be remedied by the courts. And judges must not allow themselves to be led, or indeed voluntarily wander, into areas calling for adjudication on political and non-justiciable issues. They are charged by the Constitution with exercising the judicial power of government and it would both weaken their important constitutional role as well as amount to an unconstitutional act for judges to adjudicate on such issues."

This issue was addressed again in *McKenna v An Taoiseach (No. 2)* [1995] 2 I.R. 10, where the Supreme Court implicitly disapproved of Costello J.'s finding in *McKenna (No. 1)*. In *McKenna (No. 2)*, Hamilton C.J. noted:

"Neither the powers of the Oireachtas nor of the Government are absolute even within their own domain. The Oireachtas is inhibited from enacting any law which is in any respect repugnant to the Constitution or any provision thereof and the exercise by the Government of the executive power of the State is subject to the provisions of the Constitution. They are both creatures of the Constitution and are not empowered to act free from the restraints of the Constitution. There are boundaries to their areas of activity and function. As stated by Walsh J. in the passage from *Crotty*:

'To the judicial organ of Government is given the power conclusively to decide if there has been a breach of constitutional restraints.'

Consequently, it is the right and duty of the Court to examine, and if necessary to review the activities of the Government to ascertain whether its activities are within its permitted areas of activity and function and whether the constitutional rights of the litigant are being invaded by such activity."

The Supreme Court declared that the use of public funds to promote, in a one-sided manner, a particular outcome to the referendum, was constitutionally impermissible.

Certain ministerial decisions may be susceptible to judicial review if it can be proven that they were made mala fides. In *Roncarelli v Duplessis* [1959] S.C.R. 121, a decision made by the Premier of Quebec to revoke a liquor licence granted to a Jehovah's Witness was susceptible to judicial review when it was made mala fides. The decision to revoke the licence had been based on hostility towards the Jehovah's Witness faith, and the fact that the applicant had been a particularly active member of that faith. In *Rooney v Minister for Agriculture and Food* [1991] 2 I.R. 539, the Supreme Court held that it had no power to compel a Minister to make regulations in the absence of mala fides or abuse of power.

Dudley v An Taoiseach [1994] 2 I.L.R.M. 321 related to the failure of the Dáil to hold an election. It was held that declaratory relief was not obtainable against Dáil Éireann because such relief should only be granted where it could be followed up by an enforceable order. Such an order could not be made as the courts cannot grant an order of mandamus compelling the body of members of the Dáil to vote in a particular way on a particular motion. However, Geoghegan J. noted that as Dáil Éireann cannot move of its own motion, there was an arguable case that the Government has a constitutional obligation to set down and to support motions for the holding of a by-election after a reasonable time has elapsed from the vacancy arising. As judicial review of a Minister in the exercise of his powers and functions is possible, there was an arguable case that the judicial review of the conduct of the Government could be granted in the circumstances of this case.

This case can be contrasted with the recent decision of *Doherty v Government of Ireland* [2011] 2 I.R. 222. In that case, the applicant was a Sinn Féin senator and election candidate who sought to judicially review the Government's failure to hold a by-election. The Government relied on a defence that it would breach the separation of powers if the court were to grant any relief. The High Court found that actions or omissions of the Oireachtas that affect or infringe citizens' rights under the Constitution are prima facie justiciable. This case is currently under appeal to the Supreme Court.

In *Maguire v Ardagh* [2002] 1 I.R. 385, Keane C.J. noted that the Constitution did not expressly exempt the actions of the Oireachtas or individual members thereof from judicial scrutiny, save to the extent specified in Art.15.12 and 15.13. He acknowledged that the doctrine of the separation of powers precluded the courts from accepting every invitation to interfere with the conduct by the Oireachtas of its own affairs. He listed a number of occasions where the courts cannot interfere with the Oireachtas:

> "The courts have made it clear that they will not intervene in the manner in which the House exercises its jurisdiction under Article 15.10 to make its own rules and standing orders and to ensure freedom of debate where the actions sought to be impugned do not affect the rights of citizens who are not members of the House: see the decision of this court in *Slattery v An Taoiseach* [1993] 1 IR 286. It was also held by the former Supreme Court in *Wireless Dealers Association v Minister for Industry and Commerce* (Unreported, Supreme Court, 14th March, 1956) that the courts could not intervene in the legislative function itself: their powers to find legislation invalid having regard to the provisions of the Constitution arise only after the enactment of legislation by the Oireachtas, save in the case of a reference of a Bill by the President to this court under Article 26. Nor, in general, will the courts assume the role exclusively assigned to the Oireachtas in the raising of taxation and the distribution of public resources, as more recently made clear by this court in *T.D. v Minister for Education and Science and Others* [2001] 4 IR 259."

12 Judicial Review Procedure

Introduction

Every judicial review must go through two stages. The first stage is an application for leave to apply for judicial review; the second, provided the first stage is successful, is the substantive application for judicial review. Once an applicant has been granted leave, the applicant is said to have liberty to apply for judicial review.

Application for Leave

Order 84 r.20(1) of the Rules of the Superior Courts (RSC) states: "No application for judicial review shall be made unless the leave of the Court has been obtained in accordance with this rule." The application for leave is essentially asking the court for permission to judicially review something. Applications for leave are usually brought on an ex parte basis, which means it is done by one side without the other side being present. According to Kelly J. in *O'Leary v Minister for Transport, Energy and Communications* [2000] 1 I.L.R.M. 391, the purpose of this stage is to provide the mechanism by which frivolous, vexatious or claims of no substance are weeded out, thereby preventing court time and resources from being wasted. Interestingly, there is no equivalent filtering mechanism to get rid of spurious cases in private law cases between individuals—it only exists in this public law remedy taken against State bodies. The application for leave to seek judicial review will be grounded upon a statement of grounds. This statement should concisely set out the reasons why the judicial review is being sought. It should be accompanied by an affidavit which verifies the facts behind the judicial review. A court can require the applicant's statement to be amended, setting out further and better particulars of the grounds upon which the relief is sought.

One example of a vexatious case where leave was refused arose in late October 2012. In *Garvey v President of the GAA* (2012/824 JR), a 75-year-old Louth GAA fan wanted to challenge Meath's controversial winning goal in the 2010 Leinster football final at Croke Park. Peart J. dismissed his application for judicial review as he had no arguable case and it was outside the time limits—see A. O'Faoláin, "Football fan fails to bring challenge over 2010 goal", *Irish Independent*, October 22, 2012.

In *G v DPP* [1994] 1 I.R. 374, Finlay C.J. held that an applicant for judicial review must, prima facie, satisfy the court, by the facts in his affidavit and submissions, of the following:

(a) that he has a sufficient interest in the matter to comply with Ord.84 r.20(4) of the RSC;
(b) that the facts averred in the affidavit would be sufficient, if proved, to support a stateable ground for the form of relief sought by way of judicial review;
(c) that, on those facts, an arguable case in law can be made that the applicant is entitled to the reliefs which he seeks;
(d) that the application has been made promptly and, in any event, within the time limit provided for in Ord.84 r.21(1) of the RSC; and
(e) that the only effective remedy, on the facts established by the applicant, which the applicant could obtain, is an order by way of judicial review, or, if there is an alternative remedy, that the application by way of judicial review is, on all the facts of the case, a more appropriate method of procedure.

He added that these conditions were not intended to be exclusive and that the courts have a general discretion in the granting of leave, which may include a consideration of, inter alia, whether the matter concerned was important or trivial, and whether the applicant has shown good faith in the making of an ex parte application.

An application for leave can be directed to be on notice to the respondent. This means that the respondent will be entitled to be present at the application and to make submissions on it. A question has arisen as to the appropriate standard of proof required of applicants for judicial review in such applications. Is it the normal standard of "arguable grounds" stated by Finlay C.J. in *G v DPP*? Is it the "substantial grounds" standard which applies under certain statutory areas such as asylum and planning law? Or is it a different, third test? This problem was considered by Irvine J. in *Ernst & Young v Purcell* [2011] IEHC 203. In that case, Irvine J. considered a number of cases in which there had been a suggestion that there should be a different standard of proof—in particular, the judgment of the Supreme Court in *DC v DPP* [2005] IESC 77. In that case, Denham J. (as she then was) stated:

"Reference was made in the High Court to a different standard of proof in cases where the respondent is on notice of the application. However,

I do not apply such an approach in this appeal. It appears to me that there is a real danger of developing a multiplicity of different approaches, that of *G. v. Director of Public Prosecutions*, the test applied in specific statutory schemes, and that governing the position where a respondent is on notice in a particular area of litigation. Not only may there be legal difficulties in identifying and applying each different standard, but such an approach would also take up further valuable court time. In voicing this opinion I note that in both *Gorman v. Minister for the Environment* [2001] 1 IR 306 and other cases cited reliance was placed on English case law. However, it appears to me that the appropriate law is that which was well established in this jurisdiction based on *G. v. The Director of Public Prosecutions*. It is that standard which I apply to this application."

Irvine J. followed this approach and held that the court should not apply a higher standard than the "arguable case" standard. This approach was also followed by MacMenamin J. in *CRA v Minister for Justice* [2011] IEHC 203.

One final point to note is that where the relief sought is a declaration, an injunction or damages, Ord.84 r.27(5) of the RSC provides that if the court thinks that the relief sought should not be granted in a judicial review, but might have been granted if it had been sought in a civil action begun by plenary summons by the applicant, then, instead of refusing the application, the court may order the proceedings to continue as if they had been begun by plenary summons.

Amending Grounds

It is possible to amend the grounds upon which an application for leave has been made. The principles applicable to an application to amend grounds were set out by Fennelly J. in *Keegan v Garda Síochána Ombudsman Commission* [2012] IESC 29. They may be summarised as follows:

1. the court should have regard to the interests of justice;
2. the point sought to be advanced ought to be an arguable one;
3. there should be good reason for allowing the late amendment, e.g. circumstances should be exceptional;
4. the court should consider whether the facts are new facts that arose since leave was granted;
5. the court should consider whether the proposed amendment would be a significant enlargement of the proceedings already in being;
6. the court should consider whether the proposed amendment would prejudice the respondent;

7. the court should bear in mind the true nature of judicial review; in noting that the leave stage of judicial review is a filtering mechanism, the court should consider the overarching requirement of promptness;
8. the relevance of the grounds should be considered; and
9. every case depends on its own facts.

This approach was followed by Hedigan J. in *Fleury v Minister for Agriculture* [2012] IEHC 543. In that case, he refused to allow an application to be amended eight years and nine months after a statement of opposition was served.

STATEMENT OF OPPOSITION

If a respondent intends to oppose the application for judicial review, it is required to file a statement of opposition within three weeks of being served notice of the judicial review. It can file a replying affidavit which contests the facts set out by the applicant. The statement of opposition sets out the grounds why it opposes the application for judicial review. It is not enough to simply deny everything alleged by the statement grounding the application. Instead, the respondent should state precisely every ground of opposition, giving particulars where appropriate, identifying the facts or matters supporting each ground. The respondent also has to deal specifically with every fact or matter relied upon in the statement grounding the application for judicial review which it does not admit as being true (except damages, if damages are claimed).

TELESCOPED HEARINGS

A form of judicial review hearing that is increasingly being used is the telescoped hearing. A telescoped hearing is where the court treats an application for leave to seek judicial review as also being the main judicial review hearing, thus "telescoping" the two-stage procedure into a single stage. The objective behind telescoped hearings is to save on time and expense. Telescoped hearings are particularly used in asylum cases where the applicants may have been waiting several years for a hearing and want matters to be dealt with as speedily as possible. It was pointed out in *Mulcreevy v Minister for the Environment* [2004] 1 I.R. 72 that the entirety of the case will often depend on the legal issues dealt with in the application for leave, and after they have been dealt with, there will be no outstanding issues of fact that will require their own hearing. The procedure for telescoped hearings can be found in Ord.84 r.24(2) of the RSC. Hearings can be telescoped either with the consent of the parties, or where one party applies to have the hearing telescoped, or where the court itself decides to do so. There must be good and sufficient reason to telescope the hearing, and it must be just and equitable to do so. This procedure mirrors that laid out in s.50A(2) of the Planning and Development Act 2000 (as substituted by s.32 of the Planning and Development (Amendment) Act 2010).

In telescoped hearings, the court will "case manage" the proceedings, ensuring that they are determined in a just and speedy manner which is likely to minimise costs. Case management includes the giving of directions for alerting notice parties, for the exchange of documents between the parties, and for whether the full hearing will require oral submissions or any written submissions. In *AAA v Minister for Justice* [2011] 2 I.R. 478, it was held that the respondents were entitled to decline to have a telescoped hearing, and the decision to grant leave could not thereby entitle the applicant to an award of costs.

PARTIAL LEAVE

When an application is being made for leave to judicially review a decision, there will often be a number of reasons why leave is being sought to judicially review that decision. The courts have the power to grant partial leave—that is, leave to judicially review a decision for some, but not all, of the reasons. In *Mulholland v An Bord Pleanála* [2006] 1 I.R. 453, the judge decided to grant leave on two of the grounds sought, but not on a third. Kelly J. said:

> "In the case of the first two grounds of complaint, I am of opinion that they have made out substantial grounds and ought to be given leave to apply. I am not so convinced in respect of the third. Insofar as the third ground is concerned I will give detailed reasons for so finding. But I cannot see any benefit in so doing in respect of the first two. To do so would, in many respects, be a waste of time and contrary to the approach of the High Court (Carroll J) in *McNamara v An Bord Pleanála* [1995] 2 ILRM 125. In any event, as she pointed out, the applicants are not confined in their arguments at the full hearing to those which I believe may have merit. It is sufficient therefore to state my conclusion in respect of these two grounds."

Success Rate at the Application for Leave Stage

The leave stage is intended to be a filter for frivolous and vexatious claims. The statistics issued by the Courts Service would indicate that only a minority of claims are filtered out at the leave stage. The most recent year for which such statistics are currently available is 2011. 490 applications for judicial review (in proceedings other than asylum) were received that year; of those, 400 were granted liberty to apply for judicial review and 44 were refused liberty to apply. In asylum-related cases, 703 applications were received in that year, but liberty to apply was granted in only 129 cases and was refused in only 40 cases. In 2010, 645 non-asylum-related applications were received. Liberty to apply was granted in 566 cases and refused in 59 cases. In asylum-related cases in 2010, 936 applications were received; liberty to apply was granted in 135 cases and was refused in 120 cases. The reason for the difference between asylum law and other areas of law is because judicial review is frequently used as a delaying tactic in order to keep the applicant in the country, and the cases are frequently dropped, either because the case has no merit or the applicant has received some other remedy which allows him or her to stay in the country. This is why the statistics are supplied separately.

Notice Parties

A notice party is a person who is notified about a case because, although it is not a direct party to the proceedings, it will be directly affected by it. Any person who may be affected by the judicial review proceedings and judgment should be notified, or may apply to be heard as a notice party. For example, if a person is challenging a decision by An Bord Pleanála to grant planning permission, it would be appropriate to add the person who was granted planning permission as a notice party, as the decision will affect his or her interests. A good example of this principle in practice can be seen in *BUPA Ireland Ltd v Health Insurance Authority (No. 1)* [2006] 1 I.R. 201. In that case, Bupa sought to challenge a decision by the Health Insurance Authority to recommend to the Minister for Health that certain payments be made which benefited BUPA's main competition, the VHI. The Supreme Court held it was appropriate to add the VHI as a notice party to the case as it would be affected by the outcome. In *L(MJ) v Judge Haughton* [2007] IEHC 316, a husband engaged in family law proceedings sought to judicially review the Legal Aid Board's decision to grant legal aid to his wife. She was added as a notice party to the review. In many areas of law, the serving of notice is mandatory; for example, notice must be served on the Attorney General in any proceedings wherein the constitutional validity of a law is challenged.

Amicus Curiae

An amicus curiae is another type of person who can take part in judicial review proceedings. "Amicus curiae" means "friend of the court". An amicus curiae is someone who is not a party to the case and who offers information that bears on the case, but has not been solicited by any of the parties to assist the court. In *McCann v Judge of Monaghan District Court* [2009] 4 I.R. 200 and in *Fleming v Ireland* [2013] 2 I.L.R.M. 73, for example, the Human Rights Commission was added as an amicus curiae. In *Fitzpatrick v FK* [2007] 2 I.R. 406, the High Court set out factors which should be considered before someone is added as an amicus curiae. This case involved a hospital that wished to give a blood transfusion to a Jehovah's Witness, which was against her religious beliefs. The Jehovah's Witnesses' representative body in Ireland wanted to be added to the case. It was held that, amongst the important factors to be taken into account in considering whether the court should exercise its discretion to join a party as an amicus curiae, were: (a) whether the proposed amicus curiae might reasonably be said to be partisan or largely neutral, and in a position to bring to bear expertise in respect of an area which might not otherwise be available to the court; (b) whether the proceedings were at trial or appellate stage; (c) whether the joinder of the proposed amicus curiae was likely to bring to bear—on a case involving an issue of significant public importance—a perspective or resources that might not otherwise be available; (d) whether the body seeking to be joined as an amicus curiae was charged—either in domestic or international law—with a public role in the area the subject matter of the litigation.

Application for Judicial Review

If leave to apply for judicial review is granted, the matter progresses to the next stage—the application for judicial review. This is the substantive case. The applicant has seven days from the granting of leave, or such other period as the court may direct, to serve a notice of motions or summons on the respondent. During the judicial review hearing, the parties will argue the merits of the decision and whether or not it breaches any of the principles of administrative law. The onus is on the applicant to prove, on the balance of probabilities, that the rules of administrative law have been breached. This means that the applicant has to satisfy the judge that it is more likely than not that the rule(s) was/were breached. If this is done, and the judge does not feel that any of the discretionary bars to judicial review should operate, then there are a number of remedies the judge can award the applicant.

Locus Standi

13

INTRODUCTION

If a person wishes to take a case, he must have legal standing, or locus standi, to take that case. If a person does not have sufficient standing, he is not entitled to take the case, even if it would otherwise succeed. This is true for any area of Irish law, not just administrative law. To have legal standing, one must be affected by the issues in the case. If anyone could take a case on issues which did not affect them, the courts would be overwhelmed with work and the entire legal system would be unable to function. The quality of argument would be impaired as cases are given more attention and better care if they deal with a real issue rather than a hypothetical moot point. When one is arguing a case which is not one's own, one is said to be arguing a *jus tertii.* The purpose of the locus standi rule, according to O'Higgins C.J. in *Cahill v Sutton* [1980] 1 I.R. 269, is to stop the courts from becoming "the happy hunting ground of the busybody and the crank". Originally, an applicant had to show that he was an "aggrieved person". The test now is to show that he has sufficient interest in the case in order to be allowed to take it. Order 84 r.20(5) of the Rules of the Superior Courts (RSC), as amended, now states:

> The court shall not grant leave unless it considers that the applicant has a sufficient interest in the matter to which the application relates.

DEVELOPMENT

The leading case on locus standi is *Cahill v Sutton.* In that case, the plaintiff challenged the Statute of Limitations 1957—which prevented injured parties from taking personal injuries cases three years after the date of their injury—on the ground that a person might not be aware of an injury until after the time limit had elapsed, and this was alleged to infringe that person's constitutional right to sue for damages. This did not apply to the plaintiff, as she had been aware of her injury from the beginning but had failed to take her case in time. Henchy J. said that the applicant must "show that the impact of the impugned law on his personal situation discloses an injury or prejudice which he has either suffered or is in imminent danger of suffering". Otherwise:

"If the Courts were to accord citizens unrestricted access, regardless of qualification, for the purpose of getting legislative provisions invalidated on constitutional grounds, this important jurisdiction would be subject to abuse. For the litigious person, the crank, the obstructionist, the meddlesome, the perverse, the officious man of straw and many others, the temptation to litigate the constitutionality of a law, rather than to observe it, would prove irresistible."

O'Higgins C.J. explained the purpose of the rule as follows:

"This Court's jurisdiction, and that of the High Court, to decide questions concerning the validity of laws passed by the Oireachtas is essential to the preservation and proper functioning of the Constitution itself. Without the exercise of such a jurisdiction, the checks and balances of the Constitution would cease to operate and those rights and liberties which are both the heritage and the mark of free men would be endangered. However, the jurisdiction should be exercised for the purpose for which it was conferred – in protection of the Constitution and of the rights and liberties thereby conferred. Where the person who questions the validity of a law can point to no right of his which has been broken, endangered or threatened by reason of the alleged invalidity, then, if nothing more can be advanced, the Courts should not entertain a question so raised. To do so would be to make of the Courts the happy hunting ground of the busybody and the crank. Worse still, it would result in a jurisdiction which ought to be prized as the citizen's shield and protection becoming debased and devalued."

In *State (Lynch) v Cooney* [1982] I.R. 337, Walsh J., in the Supreme Court, emphasised the need for a flexible approach to locus standi, and that each case turns on its own facts:

"The question of whether or not a person has sufficient interest must depend upon the circumstances of each particular case. In each case the question of sufficient interest is a mixed question of fact and law which must be decided upon legal principles but, it should be added, there is a greater importance to be attached to the facts because it is only by examination of the facts that the court can come to a decision as to whether there is a sufficient interest in the matter to which the application relates."

That case concerned a challenge to an order made by the Minister for Posts and Telegraphs banning RTÉ from broadcasting statements made on behalf of Sinn Féin. The applicant was a Sinn Féin election candidate. The respondent argued that none of the applicant's rights had been infringed and that, therefore, he could not be heard. The court found that the effect of the order was to deprive the applicant and his political party of a lawful benefit and that, therefore, he had locus standi to challenge the order.

The locus standi principles of *Cahill v Sutton* were approved for judicial review applications by the Supreme Court in *Lancefort Ltd v An Bord Pleanála (No. 2)* [1999] 2 I.R. 270. In that case, the applicant was a company limited by guarantee. It had been formed following the decision of An Bord Pleanála to grant planning permission to demolish Victorian-era listed buildings in order to build a hotel. The company had been founded with the purpose of challenging this decision. The company's standing was challenged on grounds that it had not participated in the planning process and it had insufficient assets to meet an award of costs against it. The Supreme Court found that a limited company may have locus standi to bring judicial review proceedings challenging a planning decision, even if the company could not point to an interest affected by the decision. It also found that the fact that a person affected by a proposed development did not participate in the planning process was not, in itself, a reason for refusing locus standi, and that a company which came into being after the decision which it was sought to challenge may have locus standi. However, the court found, on the facts, that the applicant company did not have locus standi to take this case. In *Digital Rights Ireland Ltd v Minister for Communications, Marine and Natural Resources* [2010] 3 I.R. 251, the High Court held that it is only necessary for the court, in the context of deciding locus standi, to determine that a limited company may avail of rights which were in fact infringed. It is not necessary for the court to determine the extent or breadth of those rights held by the company.

Sufficient Interest

The courts are fair as to what constitutes "sufficient interest" in a judicial review. An applicant may be granted leave even if he does not have any financial interest in a case or is not personally affected by it, provided he can show a genuine interest in challenging the lawfulness of an act or decision. In *Chambers v An Bord Pleanála* [1992] 1 I.R. 134, the Supreme Court considered the test which should be used in deciding whether or not an applicant has sufficient interest. McCarthy J. stated:

"Examination of ... the case law cited makes it clear beyond question that the issue of sufficient interest is one capable of objective assessment and relates to the impact on personal situation, ranging from the liability of a rate payer to pay his share of the cost of the luncheon had by the members of Dublin Corporation to the damage to the plaintiffs' business and the licensing provisions covered in *East Donegal Co-Operative Livestock Mart Ltd. v Attorney General* [1970] IR 317."

Sufficient interest was considered in *Digital Rights Ireland Ltd*. In that case, McKechnie J. found that where the constitutionality of a law which will affect every citizen equally is impugned, an applicant will not necessarily be denied locus standi simply because he is unable to point to any specific prejudice or injury which the law would cause him. However, in *Construction Industry Federation v Dublin City Council* [2005] 2 I.R. 496, the Supreme Court held that an applicant will be found not to have sufficient interest if there is someone in a better position to take the case. The court held that there must be:

"... good practical reasons why, in the discretion of the court, the applicant ought to be allowed to make the application. There undoubtedly are cases where administrative errors would go unchallenged if an application was refused on the grounds of *locus standi*. Clearly, consideration of this question must depend largely on the circumstances of the individual case."

This approach was followed by Kelly J. in *John Paul Construction Ltd v Minister for the Environment, Heritage and Local Government* [2006] IEHC 255. He was also of the opinion that general principles, such as were expressed in *Cahill v Sutton*, do not amount to absolute rules.

In *TD v Minister for Education* [2001] 4 I.R. 259, the applicants were young people with special needs and they were seeking to compel the State to provide high support and secure units which would meet needs generally, though not necessarily their own needs. The Supreme Court split on the issue of whether the applicants had sufficient interest. Keane C.J. and Denham J. (as she then was) found that they did; Hardiman and Murray JJ. found that they did not; and Murphy J. expressed no views, one way or the other.

SUBSTANTIAL INTEREST

The standard rule under Ord.84 r.20(5) of the RSC is that an applicant must have "sufficient interest" in order to seek a judicial review. This standard has been raised in certain areas of law, primarily planning law, by statute. In these areas, the applicant is required to have a "substantial interest" rather than a "sufficient interest". This test is used, for example, in s.47A(2)(b)(i) of the Transport (Railway Infrastructure) Act 2001, as amended. This test was originally introduced in s.50(4) of the Planning and Development Act 2000, but that provision has since been amended back to a "sufficient interest" test by s.20 of the Environment (Miscellaneous Provisions) Act 2011. Having an interest in seeing that the law is upheld is not enough to amount to a "substantial interest" according to Ó Caoimh J. in *O'Shea v Kerry CC* [2003] 4 I.R. 134. In the High Court decision of *Harrington v An Bord Pleanála* [2006] 1 I.R. 338, Macken J. considered that the substantial interest which the applicant must have is one which he has already expressed as being peculiar or personal to him. In *O'Brien v Dún Laoghaire Rathdown CC* [2006] IEHC 177, it was held that a passionate interest in the planning process is not sufficient to establish a substantial interest in it. In that case, the applicant was a member of An Taisce and was objecting to a development in her neighbourhood, but it was one which did not affect her immediate domestic environment. Substantial interest was considered by the Supreme Court in *Harding v Cork CC* [2008] 4 I.R. 318, where both Murray C.J. and Kearns J. agreed with Macken J.'s conclusion in *Harrington v An Bord Pleanála.* Murray C.J. felt that the test was that the applicant must have an interest in the decision which is peculiar and personal to him, and that the interest is significant and weighty. Kearns J. was satisfied that Clarke J., in the High Court, had identified correctly the approach to be adopted by the court in assessing whether a particular applicant has or has not got a substantial interest in a matter. The test was that:

> "The interest must be weighty and personal to the applicant in the sense that he or she has a demonstrable stake in the project, perhaps shared with others, deriving from the proximity and connectedness of his interest to the proposed development and its likely or probable effects."

The "substantial interest" test in planning cases was criticised by the European Court of Justice in *Commission of the European Communities v Ireland* (C-427/07) [2009] E.C.R. I-6277. The court criticised Ireland's failure to implement the Aarhus Convention. The 2011 changes were brought in to allow the State to ratify this Convention.

EXCEPTIONS TO THE NORMAL LOCUS STANDI RULES

The Supreme Court in *Cahill v Sutton* outlined two exceptions to the normal rules of locus standi:

1. representative cases; and
2. public interest cases.

REPRESENTATIVE CASES

The Supreme Court in *Cahill v Sutton* took into account that there may be cases where "those prejudicially affected may not be in a position to assert adequately, or in time, their constitutional rights". In a number of cases, the courts have been prepared to allow judicial review to be taken by representative bodies rather than those directly affected. Traditionally, this has not always been the case. In *R. (I.U.D.W.U. & C.) v Rathmines UDC* [1928] I.R. 260, the Supreme Court was not prepared to allow a trade union to seek an order of mandamus on behalf of its members, as the union had no standing, whereas the individuals it represented did.

In *SPUC v Coogan* [1989] I.R. 734, the Society for the Protection of Unborn Children (SPUC) sought to prevent the publication of the University College Dublin Student Union welfare guide, which contained information on abortion. The Supreme Court found that the test for locus standi in such cases was that any party who had a bona fide concern and interest in the protection of the constitutionally guaranteed right to life of the unborn had sufficient standing to take a case to defend and vindicate that right. In order to ascertain whether such bona fide concern and interest exists in a particular case, it is of special importance to consider the nature of the constitutional right sought to be protected. Finlay C.J. observed: "The threat to that constitutional right which it is sought to avoid is the death of the child. In respect of such a threat there can never be a victim or potential victim who can sue."

In *Construction Industry Federation v Dublin City Council* [2005] 2 I.R. 496, the Supreme Court held that there is no automatic entitlement for a representative group to seek judicial review. This case involved an unincorporated association representing the interest of parties involved in the construction industry. The applicant claimed to have a sufficient interest on the basis that a proposed scheme would affect all of its members and, therefore, it had a common interest with its members. However, the Supreme Court felt that to allow the applicant to argue this point without relating it to any particular application, and without showing any damage to the applicant itself, meant that the court was being asked to deal with a hypothetical situation. The challenge could have been brought by any of the members of the applicant who were affected, and they were very large and financially substantial companies that were unlikely to be deterred by the costs of mounting a challenge. Unlike many of the cases in which parties with no personal or direct interest have been granted locus standi, there was no evidence that in the absence of the challenge by the applicant, there would have been no other challenger.

In *Sandymount and Merrion Residents' Association v An Bord Pleanála* [2013] IEHC 291, the High Court refused an application to strike out judicial review proceedings on grounds, inter alia, that there was no bar to an unincorporated association seeking leave to apply for judicial review, and to continuing the judicial review to its conclusion.

Public Interest Cases

Public interest cases are ones which tackle issues of great public importance that concern fundamental rights. An applicant who does not have sufficient interest may be given permission to seek judicial review if it is in the public interest that the challenge be taken, even if the applicant is not the direct representative of those who might be affected. In *R. v Lord Chancellor, Ex p. Child Poverty Action Group* [1999] 1 W.L.R. 347, Dyson J. defined a public interest challenge as follows:

> "The essential characteristics of a public law challenge are that it raises public law issues which are of general importance, where the applicant has no private interest in the outcome of the case. It is obvious that many, indeed most judicial review challenges, do not fall into the category of public interest challenges so defined. This is because, even if they do raise issues of general importance, they are cases in which the applicant is seeking to protect some private interest of his or her own."

This definition was approved of by the Supreme Court in *Dunne v Minister for the Environment (No. 2)* [2008] 2 I.R. 775. In *Mulcreevy v Minister for the Environment* [2004] 1 I.R. 72, the decision of the Minister for the Environment to allow the M50 motorway be built on the site of Carrickmines Castle in Dublin was being challenged by an applicant who lived in Kerry. Keane C.J. explained:

> "It has been made clear in decisions of the High Court and this court in recent times that it is not in the public interest that decisions by statutory bodies which are of at least questionable validity should wholly escape scrutiny because the person who seeks to invoke the jurisdiction of the court by way of judicial review cannot show that he is personally affected, in some sense peculiar to him, by the decision … it is undesirable that invalid legislation or unlawful practices should escape scrutiny because of the absence of an indisputably qualified objector, it is also important to ensure that unfounded and vexatious challenges are not entertained."

He found that the applicant did have locus standi to take the application despite living in Kerry, as it was claimed that the motorway would irreparably damage a national monument.

In public interest cases, those directly affected by the administrative measure may be unable to litigate due to some disability and, as a result, a number of public interest cases are taken by charities or non-governmental organisations. Two types of legal issue are recognised under the public interest exception to the locus standi rule: a novel issue of general importance, or an "abuse of power or default of power". In *Iarnród Éireann v Ireland* [1996] 3 I.R. 321 Keane J. recognised that the courts were more likely to be liberal as to standing where "the nature of the constitutional challenge is such that a plaintiff will not emerge whose interests may be said to be either immediately or prospectively affected in a manner specific to him or her".

A classic example of a public interest challenge can be seen in *Crotty v An Taoiseach* [1987] I.R. 713. In that case, the applicant challenged the ratification of the Single European Act (SEA) as being contrary to Art.29.4.3° of the Constitution, which protects national autonomy in foreign affairs. The SEA was an EU Treaty which aimed to establish closer economic and political co-operation amongst EU Member States. The applicant was suing as a public interest litigant, as none of his own interests were directly affected. The Supreme Court held that Mr Crotty had locus standi to challenge the SEA when its coming into force would affect every citizen, despite his failure to prove the threat of any special injury or prejudice peculiar to him arising from the SEA. As a result of this case, every major EU treaty has to be put to the Irish people by way of referendum rather than simply being ratified by the Government.

The criteria as to when a case will be considered to be in the public interest were laid down in *SPUC v Coogan* [1989] I.R. 734. In that case, Walsh J. expressed the view that "every member of the public has an interest in seeing that the fundamental law of the State is not defeated". The criteria can be summarised as follows:

(i)   the applicant must be acting bona fide; and
(ii) the applicant must be the best qualified applicant to take the challenge.

Bona Fides

"Bona fides" means "good faith". The courts will not allow a case where the applicant is not acting in good faith. The bona fides of applicants was in issue in *McGimpsey v Ireland* [1990] 1 I.R. 110. In that case, the applicants were Ulster Unionist politicians who sought a declaration that the Anglo Irish

Agreement was contrary to Arts 2 and 3 of the Irish Constitution, which then laid claim to the entire island of Ireland on behalf of the Republic. It was argued that they did not have locus standi, as unionists would not have a bona fide interest in having the entire island of Ireland come under the control of the Republic. Barrington J. in the High Court dismissed the bona fides argument:

> "Both plaintiffs were born in Ireland and, therefore, in contemplation of Irish law, citizens of Ireland ... The present case is unusual, and there is no exact precedent governing it, but it appears to me that the plaintiffs are patently sincere and serious people who have raised an important constitutional issue which affects them and thousands of others on both sides of the Border. Having regard to these factors and having regard to the wording of the Preamble to the Constitution and of Articles 2 and 3 it appears to me that it would be inappropriate for this court to refuse to listen to their complaints."

The bona fides of the applicants was not raised in the appeal to the Supreme Court. In *Lancefort Ltd v An Bord Pleanála (No. 2)* [1999] 2 I.R. 270, Denham J. (as she then was) noted that the bona fides of a company may be a relevant factor in considering if it has locus standi, and that the corporate veil may be lifted to determine this. In that case, the applicant was not allowed to seek judicial review as it was not acting bona fide. The applicant claimed that the grant of planning permission was unlawful, as an environmental impact assessment had not been carried out, but the applicant had not objected to planning permission on that basis. In *Indaver NV v An Bord Pleanála* [2013] IEHC 11, the High Court awarded costs against an applicant who wanted to continue a judicial review when it had no bona fide belief in the case.

BEST QUALIFIED LITIGANT

An applicant will be denied locus standi to take a public interest case if there is a better qualified or more appropriate alternative litigant. Obviously, cases should be taken by the best qualified applicant. If an applicant were to challenge an administrative decision in the abstract, whilst someone else was directly affected by that administrative decision, then the latter party would clearly make a better applicant to seek judicial review, as the issues would be live rather than academic. In *L'Henryenat v Attorney General* [1983] I.R. 193, the plaintiff was the master, but not the owner, of a French fishing boat when it was arrested at sea. He was precluded from challenging the constitutionality of certain sections of the Fisheries (Amendment) Act 1978 on the basis that the owner of the vessel in question was in a position to assert his own constitutional rights and would make a better applicant. In *Riordan v Government of Ireland* [2009] 3 I.R. 745, the applicant sought, inter alia, to challenge the constitutionality of the Court of Criminal Appeal. He had never been convicted of an offence, unlike a great many other people; therefore, he did not have locus standi to take this challenge, even though it may have been a matter of public interest.

In some cases, an applicant may be better qualified to seek judicial review over those directly affected by an administrative act. For example, in *Irish Penal Reform Trust v Governor of Mountjoy* [2005] IEHC 305, the applicant (IPRT) was held to have locus standi to challenge, by way of judicial review, conditions of detention in Mountjoy Prison on behalf of prisoners. It was held that the IPRT was more capable of mounting a challenge than the prisoners:

> "[I]f the IPRT were to be denied standing, those it represents may not have an effective way to bring the issues before the court. A potential plaintiff would not be in a position to command the expertise and financial backing at the disposal of the IPRT, a less well-informed challenge might ensue and justice may not be done."

Furthermore, an individual prisoner would be restricted by the rules of locus standi from making complaints about the treatment of other prisoners. The IPRT, on the other hand, would be able to make complaints about the overall system. Similarly, in *Ward v Bus Éireann* [1997] 2 I.R. 424, allowing the National Bus and Railway Union to seek judicial review made it unnecessary to name all 600 of its members as applicants.

LOCUS STANDI IN EUROPEAN CASES

In *Lancefort Ltd v An Bord Pleanála (No. 2)* [1999] 2 I.R. 270, Keane J. observed: "The requirements of national law as to standing may in some instances have to yield to the paramount obligation on national courts to uphold the law of the European Union." The issue of locus standi in cases where issues of EU law arise was discussed in detail by McKechnie J. in *Digital Rights Ireland Ltd v Minister for Communications, Marine and Natural Resources* [2010] 3 I.R. 251, where he stated that: "A more flexible approach to locus standi may be necessary where questions of European law are raised." In support of this, he drew from a number of findings of the European Court of Justice and held that where issues of European law arise in litigation, the courts may be required to take a more liberal approach to the issue of standing so that a person's rights are not unduly hampered or frustrated. The rules on standing should be interpreted in a way which avoid making it "virtually impossible", or "excessively difficult", or even "unduly difficult" to bring challenges where issues of European law arise. The court is not automatically prevented from refusing an applicant standing where questions of European law are raised. If a court wants to grant standing on an issue of European law, but is otherwise prevented by a strict application of the rules on locus standi, the court should grant standing where to do otherwise would render the applicant's rights under EU law effectively unenforceable.

14

Time Limits and Delay

Introduction

"Time is more of the essence, more urgent, in judicial review proceedings", according to Denham J. (as she then was) in *de Róiste v Minister for Defence* [2001] 1 I.R. 190. She was explaining why the time limits for judicial review are so much shorter than the time limits in other types of actions. Delay, and the time within which a case is taken, are issues of vital importance in judicial review. The time limits in judicial review are short so as to ensure that proceedings are not brought for the convenience of the parties but to ensure that justice is done quickly. An otherwise perfect judicial review may fail if the applicant is guilty of delay. Prior to the introduction of the Rules of the Superior Courts (RSC) 1986 (S.I. No. 15 of 1986), the amount of delay that would cause a case to fail would depend on the circumstances of each individual case.

The time limits for judicial review are found in Ord.84 r.21(1) of the RSC, as amended. The current time limit for taking any type of judicial review is three months from the date when grounds for the application first arose. The time limits were recently changed by the Rules of the Superior Courts (Judicial Review) 2011 (S.I. No. 691 of 2011)—a statutory instrument which came into effect on January 1, 2012. For example, the time limit for certiorari was shortened from six months. The time limits within which applications for judicial review have to be made been standardised—previously, different remedies had different time limits. Now, regardless of what remedy is sought, one must move within three months. Until S.I. No. 691 of 2011 came into force, there was a requirement not only to move within the time limits, but also to move promptly—this requirement has now been eliminated. The courts have the power to extend the time limits if they consider that there is a good reason to do so. Delay is mainly to be taken into account at the leave stage of a judicial review application, but it may also be considered at the hearing of the application if the court is asked to do so. At the time of writing, there is no case law on the changed time limits; however, the previous case law may still be of relevance.

The reason behind the recent changes to the time limits was to speed up the courts' processes; however, it places pressure on applicants to move very quickly and there have been concerns that it will lessen the effectiveness of the remedy—particularly where delays by public bodies are common. This may even lead to a possible infringement of an applicant's rights under art.6 of the European Convention on Human Rights.

STATUTORY TIME LIMITS

In certain areas of law, the time limits for judicial review have been specifically shortened by statute. For example, the time limits in planning law and immigration law are much shorter than the three months provided for by Ord.84 of the RSC—the statutory time limits are a matter of weeks rather than months. The statutes governing these areas of law have laid out their own time limits within which judicial review can be taken, and they pre-date the changes made by S.I. No. 691 of 2011.

In planning law, the time limits within which a judicial review can be sought are governed by s.50(6) and (7) of the Planning and Development Act 2000, as substituted by s.13 of the Planning and Development (Strategic Infrastructure) Act 2006. The time limit is eight weeks.

In immigration law, the time limits within which a judicial review can be sought are governed by s.5(2)(a) of the Illegal Immigrants (Trafficking) Act 2000. The time limit is 14 days from the notification of the decision.

These are two particularly busy areas of judicial review, which may account for the shortened time limits. Decisions of the Refugee Appeals Tribunal, for example, account for 21.6 per cent of all judicial reviews sought between the years 2007 and 2011.

WHEN TIME STARTS TO RUN

It can sometimes be difficult to say when an administrative decision was made. As a result, it may be difficult to assess when time limits should start and end. Order 84 r.21(1) of the RSC indicates time starts to run "when grounds for the application first arose". When judicially reviewing a decision, the time begins to run only when a decision becomes effective, according to the Supreme Court in *Mulcreevy v Minister for the Environment* [2007] 1 I.L.R.M. 216. In *Sloan v An Bord Pleanála* [2003] 2 I.L.R.M. 61, an application to quash the board's decision to approve a motorway scheme was within the time limit. However, judicial review was refused as it was held that the challenge was really to the earlier refusal of a planning inspector to broaden the scope of a public inquiry, rather than to the board's decision to approve the motorway scheme.

An applicant seeking to judicially review the validity of an indictment is entitled to wait until it has been served, according to Geoghegan J. in *CC v Ireland (No. 1)* [2006] 4 I.R. 1.

EXTENSIONS OF TIME

Three months is a very short time within which to take a case; the time limits in other types of actions are much longer. For example, in a claim for defamation, the time limit is one year; in a claim for personal injuries, the time limit is two years; and a claim for a breach of contract can be taken within six years. The longest time limit is in an adverse possession case involving land that forms part of the foreshore owned by the Government. In that instance, the Government has 60 years to take a case before title will transfer to those seeking to adversely possess the land.

It is possible to extent the time to seek judicial review. Extensions of time are now governed by Ord.84 rr.21(3)–(5) of the RSC. They provide that the court may, on an application, extend the time limit, but only if it is satisfied that there is "good and sufficient reason" for doing so and that the delay is due to circumstances which are outside the applicant's control, or which he could not reasonably have anticipated. When considering whether there is a good and sufficient reason, the court can have regard to the effect which an extension of time might have on the respondent or a third party. In *Doherty v Referendum Commission* [2012] 2 I.R. 594, it was held that, while the applicant had delayed in bringing the challenge and the delay was at least capable of being prejudicial to the other parties, the issues raised were so important and so fundamental that the court should not refuse relief on grounds of delay. Prior to the changes made by S.I. No. 691 of 2011, there only needed to be a "good reason" to extend time. "Good and sufficient reason" is the wording used in the statutes on judicially reviewing planning and immigration decisions, and suggests a higher standard of reason is required for an extension of time. The case law relating to extension of time in those areas of judicial review provides very useful guidance.

In *Kelly v Leitrim CC* [2005] 2 I.R. 404, Clarke J. considered relevant factors in an application for an extension of time under the "good and sufficient" standard of the planning code. He gave the following non-exhaustive list of factors that courts can have regard to:

    (a)   the length of time that was specified in the statute to make such an application, as the shorter the time frame, the easier it would be to prove that, in spite of reasonable diligence, it was not possible for the applicant to comply with the time limits;

(b) whether any third party rights were affected by the delay;

(c) the fact that the absence of any prejudice to a third party would not confer on a court any wider jurisdiction to extend time;

(d) the applicant's personal responsibility for the delay in initiating proceedings;

(e) the importance of the proceedings for the applicant; and

(f) at the election of the respondent, whether the applicant had an arguable case.

In *FA v Refugee Appeals Tribunal* [2007] IEHC 290, two more factors were added:

(g) whether the applicant decided to start proceedings within the time limits or could have been expected to have been able to decide whether or not to commence such proceedings; and

(h) whether the applicant had access to legal advice during the relevant period.

These cases considered the "good and sufficient" standard before it applied to every case—a time when the specialised time limits were shorter than those in general judicial review cases. They were planning and immigration cases; however, the time limits for general judicial review were subsequently shortened and the "good and sufficient" standard now applies to all areas of judicial review. This means that it is likely that the planning and immigration case law on time limits is now even more relevant.

Order 84 r.21(6) of the RSC provides that there is nothing in the rules on extending time which prevents the court from dismissing the application for judicial review on the ground that the applicant's delay in applying for leave has caused, or is likely to cause, prejudice to a respondent or third party. This means that simply because the time limits have been extended does not mean a case is immune from being dismissed for delay.

THE OLD REQUIREMENT TO MOVE PROMPTLY

There used to be a requirement that applications for judicial review had to be brought "promptly", as well as within the time limits. Even if an application was brought within the time limits, it could still be refused if it was not brought promptly. This requirement was dropped by the 2011 changes; however, the case law in this area is still of guidance to practitioners as Ord.84 r.21(6) of the RSC preserves the court's discretion to refuse judicial review where there has been a delay which causes prejudice, either to the respondent or to a third party. Whether or not an application was taken promptly depended on all the circumstances of the case. In *State (Cussen) v Brennan* [1981] I.R. 181, the applicant was an unsuccessful candidate for a medical consultation post. The time limit was then six months and the case was taken within four months. However, he was found not to have applied promptly. The applicant had waited four months to take his case and the person who had successfully applied for the position had already resigned his job in Dublin to take up the position in Cork.

In *Dekra Éireann Teo. v Minister for the Environment* [2003] 2 I.R. 270, the decision to award the contract for the national car testing system was challenged. It was held that urgency was an essential feature of any challenge to a public procurement contract, and it was in the court's discretion to bar an application if it was not brought promptly.

The judgment of McKechnie J. in *Jerry Beades Construction Ltd v Dublin Corp* [2005] IEHC 406 is also relevant. In that case, he extended the time for the application for leave to apply for judicial review, even though there had been an 11-month delay. This was on the basis that the applicant had been justified in not issuing proceedings until it had received a comprehensive account of the planning application process from the respondent. Moreover, there were no third parties whose rights would be adversely affected and the merits of the proceedings warranted an enlargement of time.

CONCLUSION

The law relating to time limits and delay is now more certain than it was prior to the introduction of Rules of the Superior Courts (Judicial Review) 2011 (S.I. No. 691 of 2011). The time limits are now quite short, although they may be extended. There is always the risk that, to borrow the words of Budd J. in *DPP v Canavan* [2007] IEHC 46, "stringent time limits [may become] a legal heffalump-trap for the unwary". In order to avoid any difficulties with time limits, the best advice is to move as quickly as possible when seeking judicial review.

Discretionary Bars to Judicial Review

INTRODUCTION

Judicial review is a discretionary remedy. According to O'Higgins C.J. in *State (Abenglen Properties Ltd) v Dublin Corp* [1984] I.R. 381, this means that "a person whose legal rights have been infringed may be awarded *certiorari* ... but the court retains a discretion to refuse his application if his conduct has been such as to disentitle him to the relief". In *White v Hussey* [1989] I.L.R.M. 109, Barr J. observed that:

> "The relief which the applicant seeks is a discretionary remedy. It seems to me that in deciding whether or not discretion should be exercised in his favour, it is proper that I should take all of the relevant considerations into account and then decide whether further justice requires that the convictions complained of should be set aside. Similar considerations apply regarding the exercise of discretion to extend time for making the application ... in determining whether to exercise discretion in favour of an applicant who seeks to quash a conviction regard must be had also to the interest of the people of Ireland who are entitled to redress where the facts establish, or clearly imply, that the applicant was in fact guilty of the offence the subject matter of the conviction which he challenges on a technical ground that has no relevance to the merits of the claim."

In *O'Keeffe v Connellan* [2009] IESC 24, the Supreme Court held that relief by way of judicial review was discretionary and depended on the facts of individual cases. However, in the absence of specific facts disentitling an applicant to relief, a remedy would ordinarily be granted. There are a number of grounds upon which a court can exercise its discretion to refuse judicial review. These grounds do not automatically bar a judicial review application and will only be imposed at the court's discretion. They are:

- lack of candour;
- futility;
- acquiesance;

- failure to exhaust alternative remedies; and
- delay.

Delay is examined separately in the chapter on time limits (Ch.14).

LACK OF CANDOUR

An application for judicial review can be dismissed where the applicant has been dishonest or has not been totally open about his case. In *Gordon v DPP* [2002] 2 I.R. 369, Fennelly J. found that a failure to put all relevant materials before the court when making an application for leave to seek judicial review may justify the leave order being set aside. In *Adams v DPP* [2001] 2 I.L.R.M. 401, Kelly J. held that:

> "[O]n any application made *ex parte* the utmost good faith must be observed and the applicant is under a duty to make full and fair disclosure of all of the relevant facts which he knows, and when supporting evidence contains material by statement of fact or the applicant has failed to make candid disclosure the *ex parte* order may be set aside on that very ground."

In *Richardson v Judge Mahon* [2013] IEHC 118, Dunne J. explained that a duty of candour means simply that applicants have to put all their cards on the table. She also noted that a duty of candour does not lie solely with the party making the application. She followed the judgment of Clarke J. in *JRM Sports Ltd t/a Limerick Football Club v Football Association of Ireland* [2007] IEHC 67, and found the test to be applied in considering whether or not there has been a lack of candour on the part of the applicant is:

> "... [first] the extent or materiality of the matters that are misstated or omitted; secondly, whether the omissions were deliberate or accidental and thirdly, the question of whether an order should in any event be given having regard to all the circumstances of the case."

Dunne J. found that "this is not a case where it could be said that the applicant has placed all his cards on the table in relation to the application", and dismissed the application.

In *ALM (An Infant) v Minister for Justice and Equality* [2013] IEHC 203, the applicant's mother's application for judicial review had been disallowed due to her lack of candour. She claimed to be from Sierra Leone but did not inform the State that she had obtained a visa in Nigeria, or that she had attempted to enter the United Kingdom on a Nigerian Passport. The court would not allow her to challenge, on a false basis, the Minister's decision not to grant her subsidiary protection.

Futility

Judicial review will not be granted where it would be pointless or it would serve no useful purpose. In *State (Abenglen Properties Ltd) v Dublin Corp* [1984] I.R. 381, Finlay P. held that "the Court should, in its discretion, refuse to make an order of *certiorari* in a case where it is clear that the applicant can derive no benefit from it". In *Ahern v Minister for Industry and Commerce (No. 2)* [1991] 1 I.R. 462, it was held that an order of certiorari quashing the decision made by the Minister to place the applicant on compulsory sick leave, until such time as he was certified by a psychiatrist as fit for full duties, would be of no benefit to the applicant, since there was no evidence that the fact that he had been placed on sick leave would prejudice his future career. In *Barry v District Judge Fitzpatrick* [1996] 1 I.L.R.M. 512, the applicant sought to review the decisions of the three respondent District Court judges to remand him on bail for a period longer than eight days when he did not consent to it. This was unlawful; however, reviewing these decisions was futile as the eight-day period had already elapsed.

If it appears that there may be some benefit to the judicial review, no matter how slight, it will avoid being barred for futility. In *MacPharthalain v Commissioners of Public Works* [1992] 1 I.R. 111, it was held that quashing a decision to designate land as an area of international scientific interest would be of "very little" benefit to the applicants. Nevertheless, the designation was quashed as there was still some benefit to the applicants. In *State (Furey) v Minister for Defence* [1988] I.L.R.M. 89, a decision to discharge the applicant from the army was quashed, even though the period for which he had enlisted had finished. This was because the discharge may have affected his future employment prospects.

Acquiescence

Acquiescence is similar to delay. An applicant may be deemed to have acquiesced to (meaning waived his right to attack) a perceived weakness in an order affecting him. This is also known as estoppel by conduct, or waiver. This bar was recognised as far back as 1901 in *R. (Kildare CC) v Commissioner of Valuation* [1901] 2 I.R. 215. In *State (Byrne) v Frawley* [1978] I.R. 326, O'Higgins C.J. noted that "acquiescence cannot confer validity as consent cannot confer jurisdiction". However, the issue is not the validity of the order which is sought to be reviewed, but, rather, the applicant's entitlement to judicially review it. O'Higgins C.J. did also note that "acquiescence depends on knowledge". In *State (Byrne) v Frawley*, the applicant had consented to being tried in a manner which was found to be unconstitutional shortly afterwards in a separate case. Henchy J. held:

"Because the prisoner freely and knowingly elected at his trial to accept the empanelled jury as competent to try him, I consider that he is now precluded by that election from claiming that the jury lacked constitutionality."

He also stated:

"Such retrospective acquiescence in the mode of trial and in the conviction and its legal consequences would appear to raise an insuperable barrier against a successful challenge at this stage to the validity of such conviction or sentence."

In *Corrigan v Irish Land Commission* [1977] I.R. 317, Henchy J. held:

"The question was whether the two particular lay commissioners were debarred from exercising that jurisdiction by reason of their prior dealing with the case. However, this point was knowingly waived by counsel for the appellant when they elected to accept the tribunal as they found it composed on the day of the hearing."

In *Burns v Judge Early* [2003] 2 I.L.R.M. 321, the applicant sought judicial review due to problems arising out of the return for trial order which allowed him to be tried by the Special Criminal Court. These issues had come to light in a different case. The applicant had consented to being tried by the Special Criminal Court and had pleaded guilty. Ó Caoimh J. held that the applicant was in a position, at all relevant times, to raise these issues at the trial, but had not done so. In seeking to judicially review the order returning the applicant for trial, the applicant had waited seven months after the orders of conviction and sentence, and nine months after the return for trial order. Ó Caoimh J. held that it was possible to apply the term "retrospective acquiescence" to the mode of trial in this case. He was satisfied that the applicant elected to allow his trial to proceed before the Special Criminal Court and pleaded before that court where it was open to him, if he so wished, to raise a preliminary plea in relation to the jurisdiction of that court. He was satisfied that the applicant freely elected to accept the jurisdiction of the Special Criminal Court to try him. On that basis, he was satisfied that the applicant was precluded by that election from claiming that the Special Criminal Court lacked jurisdiction. This approach was expressly followed and applied by the Supreme Court in *Gorman v Martin* [2005] IESC 56. In *J & E Davy t/a Davy v Financial Services Ombudsman* [2008] 2 I.L.R.M. 507, Charleton J. noted:

"It is a principle of judicial review that where an applicant complaining of a procedure has knowingly acquiesced in the defect in respect of which a complaint is made, that the High Court may refuse relief, even though an apparent entitlement to redress is made out on the basis of a failure to follow constitutionally-mandated procedures."

This dictum was cited in *Star Homes (Midleton) Ltd v Pensions Ombudsman* [2010] IEHC 463, where the court found the applicants sat on their hands and that such acquiescence defeated the right to the remedy sought.

FAILURE TO EXHAUST ALTERNATIVE REMEDIES

An applicant may be refused relief by way of judicial review if another remedy to his problem is available. For example, one commonly available remedy to an error made by a lower court is the right of appeal. In *State (Abenglen Properties Ltd) v Dublin Corp* [1984] I.R. 381, O'Higgins C.J. stated:

"The question immediately arises of the existence of a right of appeal or an alternative remedy as to the effect on the exercise of the court's discretion. It is well established that the existence of such right or remedy ought not to prevent the court from acting. It seems to me to be a question of justice. The Court ought to take into account all the circumstances of the case, including the purpose for which certiorari has been sought, the adequacy of the alternative remedy and, of course, the conduct of the applicant. If the decision impugned is made without jurisdiction or in breach of natural justice then, normally, the existence of a right of appeal or of a failure to avail of such, should be immaterial. Again, if an appeal can only deal with the merits and not with the question of the jurisdiction involved, the existence of such ought not to be a ground for refusing relief. Other than these, there may be cases where the decision exhibits an error of law and a perfectly simple appeal can rectify the complaint, or where administrative legislation provides adequate appeal machinery which is particularly suitable for dealing with errors in the application of the code in question. In such cases, while retaining always the power to quash, a court should be slow to do so unless satisfied that, for some particular reason, the appeal or alternative remedy is not adequate."

The Supreme Court in *Buckley v Kirby* [2000] 3 I.R. 431 restated the law concerning the availability of judicial review where the applicant has failed to exhaust other available remedies. Geoghegan J. identified four separate situations which can arise:

1. the applicant both appeals to the Circuit Court and brings judicial review proceedings, and at the stage of the judicial review, the appeal has been fully or partly heard;
2. the applicant has brought an appeal and moved for judicial review in circumstances where either remedy would have been equally appropriate, but where at the stage of the judicial review, the appeal is still pending;
3. the applicant has both appealed and brought judicial review proceedings in circumstances where, at the time of the judicial review hearing, the appeal is still pending but where, in all the circumstances, an appeal, rather than a judicial review, is clearly the more appropriate remedy; and
4. the applicant has not brought an appeal at all but has gone the route of judicial review in circumstances where an appeal is much the more appropriate remedy, though it would be open to a court to grant leave for judicial review.

Geoghegan J. found that the first of these situations was covered by the decision of the Supreme Court in *State (Roche) v Delap* [1980] I.R. 170. In that case, Henchy J. found that the defect in the order in question could have been corrected by the Circuit Court judge on appeal, and that as the appeal had already opened, judicial review ought not to be granted.

Where an appeal is pending but not yet heard, and but for that fact, judicial review would quite clearly be an appropriate remedy, Geoghegan J. found that the High Court, on an application for leave, is not bound to refuse leave merely because an appeal is pending. He adopted the following view of Barron J. in *McGoldrick v An Bord Pleanála* [1997] 1 I.R. 497:

"The real question to be determined where an appeal lies is the relative merits of an appeal as against granting relief by way of judicial review. It is not just a question whether an alternative remedy exists or whether the applicant has taken steps to pursue such remedy. The true question is which is the more appropriate remedy considered in the context of common sense, the ability to deal with the questions raised and the principles of fairness; provided, of course, that the applicant has not gone too far down one road to be estopped from changing his or her mind. Analysis of the authorities referred to shows that this is in effect the real consideration."

In relation to the third situation, where both remedies of appeal and judicial review were sought and where an appeal was pending and not yet heard, and the more appropriate remedy would be an appeal, it was held that leave to apply for judicial review should be refused.

In relation to the fourth of these situations, Geoghegan J. found that it did not directly arise in this case. However, he found that where an appeal would clearly be the more appropriate remedy, an applicant ought not necessarily be granted leave to bring judicial review proceedings merely because he has not appealed. If he ought to have appealed, the court has discretion to refuse leave.

In *Stefan v Minister for Justice* [2001] 4 I.R. 203, the Supreme Court held that the availability of an alternative remedy or appeal does not bar the applicant from taking judicial review proceedings where there has been a breach of fair procedures. In *L(MJ) v Judge Haughton* [2007] IEHC 316, Budd J. refused an application for leave to judicially review the Legal Aid Board. He noted that the applicant had

> "... clung firmly to his submission that the proceedings in the District Court were not properly instituted in accordance with statutory law and his further contention that as a guardian of the children he was only obliged to respond to proceedings which had been properly instituted and that the District Court judges had both acted without jurisdiction. The application was made reasonably promptly and no point arises in relation to time. However the point does arise that judicial review is not the only effective remedy available as it was open to the applicant to appeal the decisions, each and every one of them, to the Circuit Court and to make his various points there".

See also *Bula Ltd (in receivership) v Flynn (Taxing Master)* [2000] IEHC 170, where McGuinness J. discussed the duty to exhaust alternative remedies.

16 Costs

INTRODUCTION

Litigation is a very expensive process. Cases heard by the High Court regularly run to tens of thousands of euro per day and it is not unknown for the costs of some high-profile cases to run into the millions. As a result, deciding who has to pay the costs of the legal proceedings is a vitally important issue in most cases. The high expense of taking a case is very often a barrier to administrative law cases. Costs are governed by Ord.99 of the Rules of the Superior Courts (RSC). Order 84 r.20(7) of the RSC states that if the court grants leave to apply for judicial review, it may impose such terms as to costs as it thinks fit. If costs are disputed, they can be sent to the Taxing Master for an independent decision of what the lawyers should charge in a case.

GENERAL RULE—"COSTS FOLLOW THE EVENT"

Order 99 r.1(4) of the RSC: "The costs of every issue of fact or law raised upon a claim or counterclaim shall, unless otherwise ordered, follow the event." This means that the general rule is that the costs of any case will be paid by the party that lost the case. A losing party will have to pay not only its own costs, but also the winning party's costs. This is an important factor that should be taken into consideration in every case, because legal costs have the potential to be very high. This rule encourages parties to settle matters between themselves, where possible, instead of proceeding all the way to hearing, in order to keep costs as low as possible. This rule is usually followed; however, under Ord.99 r.1(1) of the RSC, costs are always at the court's discretion, and so it is not guaranteed that the losing party will have to pay. Generally, where an applicant for judicial review is successful at the application for leave, but is unsuccessful at the substantive hearing of the case, the costs of both stages will be awarded against him (*Fynes v An Bord Pleanála* [2005] IEHC 213).

Exceptions to the General Rule

It is not always the case that costs will follow the event. It is clear that a strict adherence to this rule may result in injustice, particularly where many administrative cases are taken against large State bodies—which may have "deep pockets"—by individuals who may have little or no assets. A court can make "no order" as to costs, meaning both sides pay their own costs. The court can even award partial or full costs to the losing party if it wishes. In *Fyffes Plc v DCC Ltd* [2009] 2 I.R. 417, Laffoy J. said that costs should not follow the event if "the requirements of justice indicate the general rule should be displaced". In *Dunne v Minister for the Environment (No. 2)* [2008] 2 I.R. 775, the Supreme Court discussed the exceptions to the general rule. It found that the court has a discretionary jurisdiction to vary or depart from the general rule if, in the special circumstances of a case, the interests of justice require that it should do so. It also found that there is no pre-determined category of case which falls outside the full ambit of that jurisdiction, but if there were to be, it would be up to the legislature to so decide, and not the courts.

The Supreme Court in *Dunne* went on to hold that when a court departs from the usual rule that costs follow the event, it should do so on a reasoned basis and indicate the reasons why it is doing so. It held that it would neither be possible nor desirable to attempt to list or define all those factors that might make a court depart from the general rule—any departure from the general rule is one that must be decided by a court in the circumstances of each case. It is possible, however, to examine cases where the courts have previously departed from this rule.

Special and Unusual Circumstances

According to the Supreme Court in *Mahon Tribunal v Keena (No. 2)* [2010] 1 I.R. 33, the courts have discretion to depart from the standard costs rule where there are "special and unusual circumstances". In that case, both parties sought their costs—the defendants on the basis that they had been successful and that costs follow the event; the plaintiffs on the basis that the defendants had destroyed the documentation that was crucial to the Tribunal's inquiry. The Supreme Court ordered the defendants to pay both the High Court and Supreme Court costs as their deliberate destruction of documents had deprived the Tribunal of any effective power to conduct any meaningful inquiry and, by extension, deprived the courts of the power to give effect to any order of the Tribunal.

In *Keegan v Kilrane* [2011] 3 I.R. 813, an unsuccessful applicant was awarded 50 per cent of the costs. In that case, a judge had refused to recuse himself when he had previously acted for the accused on similar charges.

In *McG v DPP* [2009] IEHC 294, the applicant unsuccessfully sought to prohibit his trial when the prosecution disclosed a very large amount of material to him two days before his trial. Herbert J. found that this disclosure was an act of serious prosecutorial oppression that was calculated to defeat or delay justice, and he made no order as to costs.

Another example is *Hussein v Labour Court (No. 2)* [2012] IEHC 599. This case arose as a result of judicial review proceedings brought by an employer challenging the jurisdiction of the Rights Commissioner and the Labour Court to hear a claim for unpaid wages by an employee who did not have a valid work permit. The Labour Court had declined to participate in the judicial review and, instead, the employee unsuccessfully tried to resist the review. Hogan J. held that because the employee had been the victim of "appalling treatment", the court would not order costs against him, as would be the standard practice.

Public Interest Challenges

In some administrative law cases, the issues considered will be of public importance. The outcome of the case may have serious implications for the lives of the citizens of Ireland. The courts have been prepared to award costs, or a portion of the costs, in these "test cases", even where the applicant lost. The courts are also more flexible when it comes to locus standi relating to these issues. Examples of public interest challenges include *Norris v Attorney General* [1984] I.R. 36, where the applicant, David Norris, was challenging Ireland's prohibition on homosexuality, or *Crotty v An Taoiseach* [1987] I.R. 713, where the applicant challenged the ratification of the Single European Act. In the *Dunne* case, the applicant was challenging the removal of parts of Carrickmines Castle, a national monument. In *Sweetman v An Bord Pleanála* [2007] IEHC 361, the applicant was challenging the development of a bypass crossing a limestone pavement, a protected habitat in EU law.

In *McEvoy v Meath CC* [2003] 1 I.R. 208, the High Court awarded costs to the unsuccessful applicants. In his ruling on costs, Quirke J. took into account the fact that the proceedings in that case fell into a category which he described as "public interest challenges". He relied on the following description of a "public law challenge" set out by Dyson J. in *R. v Lord Chancellor, Ex p. Child Poverty Action Group* [1999] 1 W.L.R. 347:

> "The essential characteristics of a public law challenge are that it raises public law issues which are of general importance, where the applicant has no private interest in the outcome of the case. It is obvious that many, indeed most judicial review challenges, do not fall into the category of public interest challenges so defined. This is because even if they do raise issues of general importance, they are cases in which

the applicant is seeking to protect some private interests of his or her own."

Murray C.J. in *Dunne* described the description as "a succinct and useful one", although he noted that it did not involve the statement of any principle of law. He did not consider it to be definitive or exhaustive of public interest litigation involving applicants who do not seek to protect some private interests of their own. However, in *Curtin v Dáil Éireann (No. 2)* [2006] IESC 27, Murray C.J. emphasised that previous case law where costs were awarded to losing parties was of limited value, and that the award of costs was always at the court's discretion:

> "The general rule is that costs follow the event subject to the Court having a discretion, for special reason, to make a different Order. It is a discretion to be exercised in the circumstances and context of each case and is one which is so exercised from time to time.
> Counsel for all parties referred to previous decisions of this Court, and the High Court, in which a discretion was exercised to make an order concerning costs which did not follow the general rule. It would neither be possible nor desirable to lay down one definitive rule according to which exceptions are made to the general rule. The discretionary function of the Court to be exercised in the context of each case militates against such a definitive rule of exception and it is also the reason why previous decisions on such a question are always of limited value."

In *Sweetman*, Hedigan J. helpfully explained that the assessment of what was amounted to a public interest challenge was governed by two principles:

> "1. That the plaintiff or applicant concerned was acting in the public interest in a matter which involved no private personal advantage; and
> 2. That the issues raised by the proceedings are of sufficient general public importance to warrant an order for costs being made in his favour."

JUDICIAL AND QUASI-JUDICIAL IMMUNITY

In judicial review cases where it is claimed that judges and quasi-judicial bodies, such as the Labour Court or the Employment Appeals Tribunal, acted improperly or beyond their powers, costs will not be awarded against the respondent judge. Costs will never be awarded against a judge hearing the review either. In *Hussein*, the court also had to examine whether costs could be awarded against the Labour Court, either to the employer—who had successfully brought the judicial review—or to the employee who had resisted the review in the Labour Court's place. Hogan J. cited the decision of Laffoy J. in *Casey v Private Security Appeals Board* [2009] IEHC 547 and found that quasi-judicial bodies enjoy an immunity from costs where they do not resist the judicial review and where they have not acted in bad faith or with impropriety. In *Casey*, it had been found that the respondent had been in a similar position to a judge and that, as it had not acted improperly, it would not be appropriate to award costs against it. No order as to costs was made. In *F v Judge O'Donnell* [2010] 1 I.L.R.M. 198, O'Neill J. considered the issues of judicial immunity, recovery of costs and access to justice under art.6 of the European Convention of Human Rights. He held that the immunity of judges was to protect the independence of the judiciary and that the rule prohibiting costs is essential to maintaining a functioning judiciary.

Costs in Planning and Development Cases

Section 50B of the Planning and Development Acts 2000–2013 governs costs in judicial reviews relating to certain European directives—specifically, the European directives which provide for public participation in the drawing up of plans and programmes relating to the environment and/or pollution prevention and control. In judicial reviews relating to these areas, the rule is now that parties will pay their own costs. The court still has the power to award costs against a party if it considers it appropriate to do so, either because the court considers that a claim or counter-claim by the party is frivolous or vexatious, or because of the manner in which the party has conducted the proceedings, or where the party is in contempt of the court. The court can also award costs in a party's favour in a matter of exceptional public importance and where, in the special circumstances of the case, it is in the interests of justice to do so.

National Asset Management Agency

There are special costs rules in interlocutory applications involving the National Asset Management Agency (NAMA). Section 189 of the National Asset Management Agency Act 2009 provides:

> (1) At the conclusion of each interlocutory application in any legal proceedings to which this Chapter applies, the court concerned shall make orders as to costs in respect of the application and, having received submissions from the parties as to the levels of those costs, the court shall measure those costs.

(2) Costs measured under *subsection (1)* shall be enforceable against the party directed to pay those costs. If the party fails to discharge those costs within 30 days of the court order measuring those costs, the court may on the application of any party to the proceedings or of its own motion impose terms as to the continuation of the proceedings pending the discharge of the costs.

This is unusual because, whilst the High Court always had jurisdiction to measure costs, it did so very infrequently. It is now mandatory for interlocutory applications against NAMA. It does not apply, however, to final orders. This may be because the legislature feared that a number of unmeritorius cases may be taken against NAMA which might never be completed, but would cost NAMA a lot of money in legal expenses before the matters are dropped. This is a blocking mechanism against such cases.

Costs in Habeas Corpus Applications

The Attorney General's Scheme was set up to provide payment for legal costs in habeas corpus proceedings under Art.40.4.2° of the Constitution (on which, see Ch.18), which are not covered by the civil or criminal legal aid schemes. As habeas corpus cases can arise very suddenly, and because time is of the essence, this could lead to difficulties in relation to costs. Fortunately, this scheme eliminates those difficulties. The scheme is now known as the Legal Aid—Custody Issues Scheme, and covers:

1. habeas corpus applications;
2. applications for bail in the High and Supreme Courts;
3. extradition and European Arrest Warrant applications; and
4. judicial review proceedings concerning criminal matters or matters where the liberty of the person is at issue.

In order to avail of the scheme, the applicant must obtain a recommendation from the court that the scheme be applied. This must be done at the start of proceedings. In order to succeed, the applicant must satisfy the court that he is not in a position to retain legal representation unless he receives the benefit of the scheme. If a translator is required, then the costs of the translator will also be covered by this scheme.

Where a habeas corpus application is not contested, a costs offer can be made. A costs offer is an offer, made by the respondent either in writing or electronically, and not on a "without prejudice" basis, to pay the costs of the proceedings, or of a specified part of the proceedings, in a specified amount. If the offer is not accepted within the time specified, and the amount of costs

COSTS

awarded by the court is less than the sum offered, then the respondent can seek against the applicant the costs of the proceedings incurred after the offer expired. The court will not be told about this until the costs are ruled.

PRE-EMPTIVE AND PROTECTIVE COSTS ORDERS

In very rare cases, the court can award pre-emptive costs, which are costs before the case has even been heard. This type of costs order originated in *R. v Lord Chancellor, Ex p. Child Poverty Action Group* [1999] 1 W.L.R. 347, where Dyson J. found it could be awarded where a case raises public law issues that are of general importance and where the applicant has no private interest in the outcome of the case. This was adopted in Irish law by Laffoy J. in *Village Residents Association v An Bord Pleanála (No. 2)* [2000] 2 I.R. 321. She held that such a costs order can be awarded where "the issues raised on the challenge [are] of general public importance". It is difficult to prove in a public interest case that the applicant has no private interest in the outcome of the case. Whilst the order was confirmed as existing in both *R. v Lord Chancellor, Ex p. Child Poverty Action Group* and *Village Residents Association v An Bord Pleanála (No. 2)*, it was not granted in either case as the applicants were found to have a private interest in the outcome of the respective decisions.

In *Friends of the Curragh v An Bord Pleanála* [2009] 4 I.R. 451, protective costs orders were discussed. Protective costs orders are similar to pre-emptive costs orders; however, they can be awarded at any stage of the proceedings. In that case, Kelly J. held that the principles governing protective costs orders were as follows:

(1) A protective costs order can be made at any stage of the proceedings, on such conditions as the court thinks fit, provided that the court is satisfied that:
   (i) the issues raised are of general public importance;
   (ii) the public interest requires that those issues should be resolved;
   (iii) the applicant has no private interest in the outcome of the case;
   (iv) having regard to the financial resources of the applicant and the respondent, and to the amount of costs that are likely to be involved, it is fair and just to make the order; and
   (v) if the order is not made, the applicant will probably discontinue the proceedings and would be acting reasonably in so doing.

(2) If those acting for the applicant were doing so pro bono, this would be likely to enhance the merits of the application for a protective costs order.

(3) It is for the court, in its discretion, to decide whether it is fair and just to make the order in the light of the considerations set out above.

Costs and Notice Parties

A court can grant costs in favour of a notice party, even if the case is discontinued (see *Eircom Plc v Director of Telecommunications Regulation* [2003] 1 I.L.R.M. 106). Generally, if an applicant for judicial review is successful, a notice party to a judicial review will bear his own costs, and costs will not be awarded against him—*Taylor (Salesian Sisters) v Shannon Explosives Ltd*, unreported, High Court, Carroll J., May 27, 2003. Where the applicant has been unsuccessful, the court will assess whether the notice party was a necessary party to the proceedings and whether he had to defend his interests. If he was, then he may have costs awarded in his favour. In *O'Connor v Nenagh District Council* [2002] IESC 42, costs had been awarded to a notice party. The Supreme Court upheld this decision as it had been appropriate to join the notice party to the case. In *Usk and District Residents Association Ltd v Environmental Protection Agency* [2007] IEHC 30, Clarke J. did not see any basis for treating a notice party differently to a respondent when it came to costs against an unsuccessful applicant. This was because the notice party was directly involved in the defence of his legitimate interests. However, he noted that:

> "The mere fact that the party may have a sufficient interest so as to make it legitimate that they be placed on notice of proceedings does not, of itself, necessarily carry with it an entitlement to that party to an unquestioned order for costs in the event of the proceedings being successfully defended."

An unsuccessful respondent's liability for costs to a notice party has also been considered. In *North Wall Property Holding Co Ltd v Dublin Docklands Development Authority* [2009] IEHC 11, Finlay Geoghegan J. held that the costs between the notice party and the respondent are in the discretion of the court, and there is nothing in Ord.99 of the RSC which applies any presumption or ordinary rule in respect of a notice party's costs.

COSTS

The European Commission has been critical of the costs in an Irish judicial review, particularly in relation to environmental matters. In *Commission of the European Communities v Ireland* (C-427/07) [2009] E.C.R. I-6277, the European Court of Justice found that art.10a of the Environmental Impact Assessment Directive (Directive 85/337 [1985] OJ L175/40), as inserted by Directive 2003/35 [2003] OJ L156/17 and as now found in art.11(4) of Directive 2011/92 [2011] OJ L26/1, set out a mandatory requirement on all Member States that the procedures for challenging decisions under the Directive must not be prohibitively expensive. More importantly, it found that the current rules and procedures in Ireland fail to fulfil this obligation. Advocate General Kokott accepted the argument that the court had discretion not to impose a costs order, but noted that this was only a discretion. She also found the argument that there is no applicable ceiling as regards the amount that an unsuccessful applicant will have to pay was a well-founded argument. The Court of Justice found that the discretionary power of the Irish courts to award costs to an unsuccessful applicant provides insufficient protection for prospective applicants, and cannot be regarded as a valid implementation of the obligations arising from art.10(a) of the Directive. Ireland is required, pursuant to art.260 of the Treaty on the Functioning of the European Union, to take the necessary measures to comply with this judgment. In *Commission v Italy* (C-69/86) [1987] E.C.R. 773, the Court of Justice found that such action needed to be "set in motion immediately and be completed in the shortest possible period". Ireland subsequently introduced s.50B of the Planning and Development Act 2000, discussed above, to remedy this. Unfortunately, this only applies to environmental and planning matters, and does not remedy the issue in other areas of law.

Judicial Review—Remedies 17

A person seeking judicial review is doing so because he wants a solution to his problem. If no remedies were available, then administrative law would be effectively pointless. There are a number of separate remedies that can be granted in a judicial review. They are governed by Ord.84 of the Rules of the Superior Courts (RSC). An applicant is not limited in the number or combination of remedies he can seek. A number of remedies—such as certiorari and mandamus—are known by their old Latin names. In England, these names have been abandoned and they are known as a quashing order and a mandatory order, respectively. This chapter will explain the most common remedies which can be granted in judicial review. One remedy—habeas corpus—will be examined separately, as it has its own procedure.

CERTIORARI

Certiorari is an order which quashes (or cancels) a decision of an administrator. It restores the parties to their positions prior to the making of the order. According to the most recent statistics released by the Courts Service, this is by far the most frequently sought remedy in judicial review: 471 cases were taken in 2010 (the most recent year for which statistics are currently available) seeking certiorari. The second most popular remedy was mandamus, with 63 cases taken seeking that remedy.

The judgment of O'Higgins C.J. in *State (Abenglen Properties Ltd) v Dublin Corp* [1984] I.R. 381 provides the history of certiorari. The remedy of certiorari first emerged in the early years of the seventeenth century and was used by the Court of King's Bench to supervise and control the use of jurisdiction of local courts run by Justices of the Peace. The court was concerned that these justices would exercise their functions properly and that there would be a uniform administration of the law throughout the country. O'Higgins C.J. went on to explain:

> "From this emergence three centuries ago ... the remedy of certiorari has been developed and extended to reach far beyond the mere control of judicial process in courts as such. To-day it is the great remedy available to citizens, on application to the High Court, when anybody

or tribunal (be it a court or otherwise), having legal authority to affect their rights and having a duty to act judicially in accordance with the law and the Constitution, acts in excess of legal authority or contrary to its duty. Despite this development and extension, however, certiorari still retains its essential features. Its purpose is to supervise the exercise of jurisdiction by such bodies or tribunals and to control any usurpation or action in excess of jurisdiction. It is not available to correct errors or to review decisions or to make the High Court a court of appeal from the decisions complained of. In addition it remains a discretionary remedy."

In *Stefan v Minister for Justice* [2001] 4 I.R. 203, Denham J. (as she then was) stated:

"*Certiorari* may be granted where the decision maker acted in breach of fair procedures. Once it is determined that an order of *certiorari* may be granted, the court retains a discretion in all the circumstances of the case as to whether an order of *certiorari* should issue. In considering all the circumstances, matters including the existence of an alternative remedy, the conduct of the applicant, the merits of the application, the consequences to the applicant if an order of *certiorari* is not granted and the degree of fairness of the procedures, should be weighed by the court in determining whether *certiorari* is the appropriate remedy to attain a just result."

MANDAMUS

Mandamus is an order which forces a party to do something. An order of mandamus compels the respondent to carry out a particular obligatory act which applies to its office or duty. Mandamus arises where an administrator has failed to take some action. Often, where the High Court has quashed the decision of a lower court with an order of certiorari, it will use an order of mandamus to compel the lower court to reconsider the proceedings. Before an application for mandamus, the applicant must first call on the administrative body concerned to do its duty, and the body must refuse. The courts do not insist on this requirement when refusal can be inferred from the surrounding circumstances (*Point Exhibition Theatre v Revenue Commissioners* [1993] 2 I.R. 551), or if it is unsuitable to make the request (*R. v Hanley Revising Barrister* [1912] 3 K.B. 518). The courts will not grant mandamus where another "equally effective and convenient remedy" exists, according to Gibson J. in *R. (Tipperary North Riding and South Riding CCs) v Considine* [1917] 2 I.R. 1. The courts will also refuse mandamus if the order is premature (*DPP v Early* [1998] 3 I.R. 158) or would serve no useful purpose (*Brady v Cavan CC* [1999] 4 I.R. 99). Mandamus is unaffected by the death, resignation or removal from office of the respondent, as the order will continue against his successor (Ord.84 r.27(6) of the RSC).

QUO WARRANTO

Quo warranto is a very rarely used remedy. It requires someone in a position of public authority to show or to establish his authority to hold that position. The Law Reform Commission has twice recommended that this remedy be abolished, but it still remains. It should also be noted that proceedings for a declaration and an injunction would achieve the same result as this remedy.

PROHIBITION

Prohibition is a preventative order that prohibits a public body from taking an action. It restrains a lower court or tribunal from exercising a jurisdiction it does not have. It can be seen as the opposite of mandamus. In *East Donegal Co-Operative Livestock Mart Ltd v Attorney* General [1970] I.R. 317, Walsh J. noted:

> "Rights which are guaranteed by the Constitution are intended to be protected by the provisions of the Constitution. To afford proper protection, the provisions must enable the person invoking them not merely to redress a wrong resulting from an infringement of the guarantees but also to prevent the threatened or impending infringement of the guarantees and to put to the test an apprehended infringement of these guarantees."

He had previously found in *State (Stephen's Green Club) v Labour Court* [1961] I.R. 84 that:

> "It is well established in this country that prohibition may issue to any body which has the duty to act judicially and which on consideration of facts and circumstances has power by its determination within its jurisdiction to impose liability or to affect rights."

Prohibition is similar to certiorari except that it is sought before something is done, rather than afterwards. It is a matter of timing—there is no need to wait to suffer an injury if it can be prevented. Prohibition is most commonly sought where the applicant seeks to prohibit a criminal trial from proceeding on the grounds that there is a real or serious risk the trial will be unfair (see *D v DPP* [1994] 2 I.R. 465). In *State (O'Connell) v Fawsitt* [1986] I.R. 362, Finlay C.J. observed:

> "I am satisfied that if a person's trial has been excessively delayed so as to prejudice his chance of obtaining a fair trial, then the appropriate remedy by which the constitutional rights of such an individual can be defended and protected is by an order of prohibition. It may well be that an equal remedy or alternative remedy in summary cases is an application to the justice concerned to dismiss because of the delay."

INJUNCTION

An application for an injunction can be made by way of an application for a judicial review. An injunction is an equitable remedy that requires a party to do, or not to do, specific acts. Injunctions can be either *interlocutory*, meaning that they last until the case is heard, or *perpetual*, meaning that they last forever. Section 28(8) of the Supreme Court of Judicature (Ireland) Act 1877 provided that the court was empowered to grant interlocutory relief "whenever it was just and convenient to do so". Order 84 r.18(2) of the RSC now states:

> An application for a declaration or an injunction may be made by way of an application for judicial review, and on such an application the Court may grant the declaration or injunction claimed if it considers that, having regard to—
> (a) the nature of the matters in respect of which relief may be granted by way of an order of mandamus, prohibition, certiorari, or quo warranto,
> (b) the nature of the persons and bodies against whom relief may be granted by way of such order, and
> (c) all the circumstances of the case, it would be just and convenient for the declaration or injunction to be granted on an application for judicial review.

This is very similar in its language to that used by the Supreme Court of Judicature (Ireland) Act 1877.

DECLARATION

As set out above, an application for a declaration can be made by way of an application for judicial review. A declaration is a judgment by the court which clarifies the rights and obligations of the parties to the proceedings, without actually making any order. According to Walsh J. in *Transport Salaried Staffs' Association v CIÉ* [1965] I.R. 180, the courts will not grant declaratory relief unless there is a substantial question which one person has a real interest to raise and the other to oppose. Unlike the remedies of certiorari, mandamus or prohibition, a declaration does not tell the parties to do anything. A judicial review seeking a declaration will often be accompanied by the other administrative remedies, most commonly certiorari.

For example, if the court declared that a proposed decision by An Bord Pleanála was unlawful, a declaration would resolve the legal position of the parties to the proceedings. If An Bord Pleanála was to continue with the rule, thereby ignoring the declaration, the applicant who obtained the declaration would not have to comply with the decision and would have the other administrative remedies available to him. This can be seen from the judgment of Costello J. in *O'Donnell v Dún Laoghaire Corp* [1991] I.L.R.M. 301, where he held:

> "A declaratory judgment is one which declares the rights of the parties and because defendants, and in particular public bodies, respect and obey such judgments they have the same legal consequences as if the court were to make orders quashing the impugned orders and decisions."

In that case, the applicants successfully sought a declaration that their water supply had been wrongfully disconnected. The rules governing the granting of declarations are found in Ord.84 r.18 of the RSC. They are the same as the rules governing the granting of injunctions laid out above.

DAMAGES

Where a person has suffered a wrong, it is the court's duty to ensure, insofar as is possible, that the wrong is corrected. One of the most common ways a court does this, in any area of Irish law, is by awarding damages to the injured party. Damages are compensation in money for the wrong suffered. Before the introduction of the RSC in 1986, it was not possible to claim damages in judicial review proceedings, and separate legal proceedings would have to be commenced in order to claim damages. One English case which illustrates the difficulties this caused is *R. v Home Secretary, Ex p. Dew* [1987] 1 W.L.R. 881. In that case, a prisoner sought an order compelling prison authorities to provide him with medical treatment. At the same time, he sought damages for negligence. After the initial ex parte application for judicial review had been made, the respondent prison authorities undertook to provide the medical treatment sought. All that was left to rule on was the applicant's claim for damages. The judge ruled that the claim for damages did not then arise from public law and he struck out the judicial review proceedings. This approach changed with the introduction of the RSC. Order 84 r.25 of the RSC now provides that on an application for judicial review, the court may award damages to the applicant if:

(a) he has included in the statement in support of his application for leave ... a claim for damages arising from any matter to which the application relates, and

(b) the Court is satisfied that, if the claim had been made in a civil action against any respondent or respondents begun by the applicant at the time of making his application, he would have been awarded damages.

In addition, Ord.19 rr.5 and 7 of the RSC apply to the statement for the claim for damages. These rules require the applicant to set out the particulars of the wrongdoing alleged, and the particulars of any items of special damages, in the same way as would be necessary in any ordinary civil action.

Habeas Corpus and Article 40 Procedure

Introduction

Habeas corpus is probably the most famous remedy in administrative law. Translated, it means "May you have the body". When using this remedy, the courts demand that people in detention be brought before them in order to inquire into the legitimacy of their detention. It is a fundamental principle of the common law that no person's liberty may be taken away from him unless every legal requirement of due process has been strictly complied with (*McIlraith v Grady* [1968] 1 Q.B. 468). This remedy dates to at least the Magna Carta of 1215 but there is some evidence that it even pre-dates this. In *R. v Knowles, Ex p. Somersett* (1772) 20 State Tr. 1, an American slave in England was ordered to be freed as "The air of England has long been too pure for a slave, and every man is free who breathes it". Habeas corpus is enshrined in the U.S. Constitution and the U.S. Supreme Court declared, in *Fay v Noia* 372 U.S. 391 (1963), that: "There is no higher duty than to maintain [habeas corpus] unimpaired." More recently, in *Linnett v Coles* [1987] Q.B. 555, Lawton L.J. in the English Court of Appeal claimed: "The writ of habeas corpus is probably the most cherished sacred cow in the British Constitution." In England, the main source of habeas corpus is the Habeas Corpus Act 1679; in Ireland, it is the Constitution.

One famous historical example which illustrates this remedy is *Ex p. Daisy Hopkins* (1891) 61 L.J.Q.B. 240. In that case, the release was ordered of the 17-year-old Daisy Hopkins. She had been convicted by the Vice-Chancellor of Cambridge University of the offence of "walking with a member of the University"—a euphemism for prostitution—and was sentenced to 14 days in the local workhouse. There was evidence that she had worked as a prostitute before, although there was no evidence she was soliciting at the time of the offence in question. The unfairness of the case led to public outcry. The Lord Chief Justice pointed out:

> "Nobody would suppose that a person simply walking with a member of the University, who might be that member's mother, or sister, or wife, or friend, was guilty of an offence against the law which would justify the Vice Chancellor in imprisoning him or her."

Even though it was recognised by everyone that she was really being tried for what Lord Coleridge called "the far graver charge of her being a person of immoral character and for having been guilty of immoral conduct", this was not enough to sustain the conviction. The conviction was quashed and she was released.

HABEAS CORPUS IN IRELAND

Habeas corpus is so fundamentally important that it is enshrined in Art.40.4.2° of our Constitution. This text replaced the pre-existing common law on habeas corpus (*Re Zwann* [1981] I.R. 395) and is also known as an "Article 40 inquiry". Order 84 r.1(2) of the Rules of the Superior Courts states that the expression "order of habeas corpus" does not include an order made pursuant to Art.40.4.2° of the Constitution, although in practice, the terms are used interchangeably. This is the only legal procedure laid out in its entirety within the Constitution. The text of Art.40.4.2° reads:

> Upon complaint being made by or on behalf of any person to the High Court or any judge thereof alleging that such person is being unlawfully detained, the High Court and any and every judge thereof to whom such complaint is made shall forthwith enquire into the said complaint and may order the person in whose custody such person is detained to produce the body of such person before the High Court on a named day and to certify in writing the grounds of his detention, and the High Court shall, upon the body of such person being produced before that Court and after giving the person in whose custody he is detained an opportunity of justifying the detention, order the release of such person from such detention unless satisfied that he is being detained in accordance with the law.

ADVANTAGES

The Article 40 procedure has a number of advantages over other adminis-trative law remedies:

1. It is a speedy remedy. Habeas corpus applications can be heard at any time of the day, even evening time and weekends. Applications have sometimes been heard at the homes of judges. In *Barry v Waldron*, unreported, High Court, Carney J., May 23, 1996, Carney J. said that he

was frequently required to hear applications out of normal hours in his own home and was once asked to sit at 05.20 to prevent someone being put on an aeroplane. He also noted that this is the only procedure in the entire law where a person is entitled to actually select the judge whom he wishes to hear the proceedings.

2. Article 40 applications take priority over all other High Court business and are very flexible in their nature. The High Court is bound to hear an inquiry once it has directed one. In *Sheehan v Reilly* [1993] 2 I.R. 81, Finlay C.J. noted that an Article 40 inquiry must necessarily transcend the normal procedural rules for application for judicial review, as it is so urgent and important. Applications which raise an issue as to the legality of the detention of a person must be treated as an application under Art.40, no matter how they are described. According to Edwards J. in *Devoy v Governor of Portlaoise Prison* [2009] IEHC 288, the court has an inherent jurisdiction to convert a misdirected application for an inquiry under Art.40.4.2° into judicial review proceedings, and vice versa.

3. The onus of proof that the detention is legal is on the detainer; the applicant is not required to show that he is unlawfully detained in order to succeed.

4. Release is a mandatory remedy, not a discretionary one. If the judge is not satisfied that the detention is lawful, he must order the release of the prisoner. Other administrative remedies are discretionary and can be refused for reasons such as delay. This was recently re-emphasised by the Supreme Court in *Caffrey v Governor of Portlaoise Prison* [2012] IESC 4. However, in *Re Singer (No. 2)* (1960) 98 I.L.T.R. 112, the applicant was arrested literally as he stepped out of Mountjoy prison, after being released following an Article 40 inquiry, by Gardaí who were waiting at the prison gates. This was held not to violate the order for release.

5. There is a source of funding specifically for habeas corpus, known as the Legal Aid—Custody Issues Scheme (formerly the Attorney General's scheme). It may be the case that lawyers acting for the prisoner are not officially instructed by him, as he is in custody, which may have caused problems with fees but for the existence of this scheme.

6. As the entire procedure is laid out in the Constitution, it cannot be eroded by Government Ministers. The only way it can be changed is by a referendum. As a result, it has remained simple and unchanged since 1937 and is not at risk of being watered down.

Article 40 inquiries are common in practice as a result of these advantages. A leading example of this procedure in action is *State (Trimbole) v Governor of Mountjoy Prison* [1985] I.R. 550. In that case, the High Court ordered the release of an Australian when it found that there was no ground supporting the allegations that he had been in possession of firearms. The real reason he was arrested was that the arrest was at the request of the Australian Government who were seeking his extradition on a series of charges, including murder and drug dealing. There was no extradition arrangement at that time between the Governments of Ireland and Australia, but it was being completed whilst he was in custody on the firearm charge. The charges and detention were an excuse to stop him from escaping before the extradition treaty was completed.

In *Kadri v Governor of Wheatfield Prison* [2012] IESC 1, the applicant was an Algerian who was resisting attempts by the Gardaí to repatriate him. Whilst en route to the airport, he vomited on the Gardaí in the Garda car, threatened to kill himself, and attempted to injure himself by bashing his head against a car window and the ground at the airport. The Gardaí bringing him to the airport realised that it would be impossible to deport him and took him back to Wheatfield prison so he could be detained whilst it was decided what to do with him. Unfortunately for the Gardaí, the statutory eight-week period within which the State had to repatriate him elapsed whilst he was in Wheatfield prison. The Supreme Court noted that he had behaved appallingly but his detention was still clearly unlawful and ordered his release.

PROCEDURE

The procedure for a habeas corpus application is straightforward and is found in the text of Art.40.4.2° of the Constitution. A complaint is made to the High Court or a judge of the High Court by way of an ex parte application grounded on an affidavit setting out the facts. Article 40 inquiries are so important that the High Court has, in the past, waived the normal strict formalities requiring an affidavit and has acted on unsworn letters, even ones which did not seek an inquiry. Once a judge decides that an inquiry is needed, the court will make an order for the production of the body of the person the subject of the application, and will require the respondent to certify in writing the grounds of the detention.

When the prisoner is produced, arguments will be heard as to whether or not the detention is lawful. This is known as the return stage. If the court finds that the detention is not lawful, it must order the release of the prisoner. The burden of proof rests on the person seeking to claim the detention is valid. Article 40.4.2° provides that the High Court judge is to order the release of the person "unless satisfied that he is being detained in accordance with law". Article 40 inquiries must be heard in open court and should not be held in camera (*XY v Clinical Director of St Patrick's University Hospital* [2012] IEHC 224).

An application can be moved in front of any High Court judge and the applicant has the right to choose which judge will hear the application. In *Joyce v Governor of the Dóchas Centre* [2012] IEHC 326, an Article 40.4.2° application had been refused by Hedigan J. and was brought again the next day in front of Hogan J. It was held that the application can be renewed before a second judge without being regarded as abusive. The second judge hearing the application must pay close attention to the reasons given by the first judge for refusing it, although he is not strictly bound by that refusal.

Who Can Make the Complaint?

Anyone can make a complaint concerning the lawfulness of detention—it is not limited to the detainee or his legal representatives. Others who can make the complaint include (but are not limited to): family members (*O'H v HSE* [2007] 3 I.R. 177); fellow prisoners (*Application of Woods* [1970] I.R. 154); political activists (*McGlinchey v Governor of Portlaoise Prison* [1988] I.R. 671); and employers (*State (Harrington) v Garda Commissioner*, unreported, High Court, Finlay P., December 14, 1976). However, third parties cannot make a complaint. Gavan Duffy J., in *State (Burke) v Lennon* [1940] I.R. 136, said that he would "not endorse an interpretation of Article 40.4.2° which would permit an application by a third party where the party detained could make the application himself". In *Application of Woods*, the judge refused to entertain an application submitted by a third party on the grounds that there was no evidence that the prisoner had ever authorised the third party to act on his behalf. This rule may be ignored where the prisoner is unable to appear himself due to his detention. In *Dolphin v Governor of the Central Mental Hospital*, unreported, High Court, Kenny J., January 27, 1972, an application had been taken on behalf of a Maoist student who had been arrested for attacking Gardaí at the opening of the University College Dublin Arts Block by the then President, Éamon de Valera. He had been committed to the Central Mental Hospital on grounds that he was unfit to plead. Kenny J. held the third parties' application acceptable, despite the fact that the prisoner did not recognise the courts due to his political beliefs. In *State (Quinn) v Ryan* [1965] I.R. 70, an enquiry was allowed despite the fact that the prisoner didn't know it was happening.

Detention

A prisoner does not necessarily have to be locked in a prison cell to be considered to be in detention. In *State (Rogers) v Galvin*, *Irish Times*, October

20, 1980, an injured suspect was under Garda supervision while in hospital and the evidence was that the Gardaí intended to arrest the applicant once he tried to discharge himself. The court held that this was detention even though he was free to leave. He was under constant surveillance and the Gardaí would have arrested him as soon as he left; therefore, he was in custody. It should be noted that this ruling was later overturned by the Supreme Court on other grounds.

These cases will turn on their own facts. In *O'Shea v Garda Commissioner* (1980) 2 Frewen 57, the applicant was similarly under 24-hour Garda surveillance in hospital, following a shoot-out with Gardaí. The court held that he was not in custody:

> "In the present case there is a finding of fact that the applicant remained of his own volition and not from any restraint imposed by the Gardaí. The fact he was aware that when he left hospital he would be arrested does not affect the Court's finding that he was not in custody."

Unfair Procedures

The case of *Nasiri v Governor of Cloverhill Prison* [2005] IEHC 471 saw the Article 40 enquiry being used as a mechanism to inquire into the fairness of procedures and level of justice afforded to an individual in the District Court. In that case, the High Court found that the District Court procedures were "in essence unfair". Prior to this case, it was assumed that in order to challenge the manner in which a District Court judge had conducted a hearing, it was necessary to bring judicial review proceedings. Article 40.4 can now be used as a mechanism to challenge a District Court decision on the grounds of the unsatisfactory manner in which the District Court judge conducted the hearing. An Article 40 inquiry is more appropriate than judicial review when a person has been deprived of liberty as a result of unfair procedures. A person should not have to wait in custody for justice to be done in his case, when he can be released.

Illegal Detention and Convicted Prisoners

The level of illegality attaching to a convicted prisoner's detention is important. A prisoner will be released only if his detention is illegal to the point where the detention is wanting in the fundamental legal qualities which are constitutionally required. In *State (McDonagh) v Frawley* [1978] I.R. 131, it was held by the Supreme Court that in order for a convicted prisoner to successfully rely on Art.40.4.2°, he must prove a breach of a fundamental requirement of the law. In that case, the prisoner was suffering from back ache in prison and claimed that he was not receiving adequate medical treatment and that his constitutional rights were being infringed as a result. His detention was found not to be illegal, although the detention of someone with similar circumstances, who was not yet convicted, could be illegal. In *Brennan v Governor of Mountjoy Prison* [1999] 1 I.L.R.M. 190, Budd J. considered that an intentional violation of a prisoner's rights might be a ground for ordering the release of a convicted prisoner in an Article 40.4.2° application. In *Ejerenwa v Governor of Cloverhill Prison* [2011] IESC 41, the applicant's detention was found to be illegal as the warrant committing him into custody was defective—it did not state on its face the reasons for his arrest and detention. In *Kinsella v Governor of Mountjoy Prison* [2011] IEHC 235, this procedure was used to litigate a prisoner's poor living conditions. The applicant was kept in solitary confinement in a 3x3m padded cell without a television, radio or reading materials, and only a cardboard box to relieve himself in. Hogan J. found that the applicant's constitutional rights had been breached, but the breach had not been so serious as to render the detention illegal. See also *Foy v Governor of Cloverhill Prison* [2010] IEHC 529.

A HISTORICAL POINT OF INTEREST

There is one final point to note on the English Habeas Corpus Act 1679. This Act is the foundation of much of the common law on habeas corpus, but was barely passed when voted on by Parliament. When the votes were counted, one Lord was jokingly counted as being worth 10 votes because he was very fat. The fact that this was a joke was missed by the inattentive tallyman. As a result, the Act was passed by a margin of two votes—57 in favour and 55 against—a total of 112 votes being cast out of a possible 107. Almost three-and-a-half centuries later, this Act is still in force in England.

Index

European cases, 106, 107
exceptions to rules, 101
public interest cases, 103
    best qualified litigant, 105
    bona fides, 104
representative cases, 102
substantial interest, 100
sufficient interest, 99, 100

Natural justice, 3, 6–8, 13–14, 18, 30, 33–34, 39, 49, 83, 117

Proportionality, 19, 42–46, 57–64
defined, 57
least restrictive means, 60
impact on rights, 61
proportionality or *Heaney* test, 58–59, 64
protected right, 63
rational connection, 59

Reasonably, duty to act, 39–46, 57, 59, 63
Wednesbury principles (or unreasonableness), 21, 39–41
    Stardust tribunal, 40
"anxious scrutiny" test, 42
court interference, 41
basis of irrationality, 41
"*Keegan/O'Keeffe*" test, 41
Meadows v Minister for Justice test for unreasonableness, 42–45, 51, 59, 63

non-refoulement, 42
proportionality principle, 42, 45, 57, 63,
Reasoned decision, 47–56
Constitutional justice, 48–53
Freedom of Information Act 1997, 53–54, 56
level of detail required, 55
Respondent, 5, 32
Rule against bias, 11, 19, 25–32
apprehension of bias, or hostility, 28
automatic bias, 25
defined, 25
objective bias, 27
political views, 31
pre-determination, 29
previous lawyer/client relationship, 31
prior involvement in disputes, 28
relationship between judge and counsel, 30
subjective (or active) bias, 26

Ultra Vires, 4, 20–24, 40, 73 *see also* **Legitimate expectation**
administrator's power, 20
Circuit and District Court jurisdictions, 21
defined, 20
doctrine, 21
legislative provisions, 21
legitimate expectation, 73
limits on power, 20